porch
&deck
Decorating Ideas & Projects

Better Homes and Gardens® Books
Des Moines, Iowa

Better Homes and Gardens® Books
An imprint of Meredith® Books

Porch & Deck Decorating Ideas & Projects
Editor: Linda Hallam
Design: The Design Office of Jerry J. Rank
Contributing Writer: Louis Joyner
Contributing Photographer: Emily Minton
Contributors: Brian Carter, Lynn McBride, Lynn Nesmith, Katie Stoddard
Copy Chief: Terri Fredrickson
Managers, Book Production: Pam Kvitne, Marjorie J. Schenkelberg
Contributing Copy Editor: Chardel Blaine
Contributing Proofreaders: Sherry Hames, Beth Lastine, Ann Marie Sapienza
Indexer: Kathleen Poole
Electronic Production Coordinator: Paula Forest
Editorial and Design Assistants: Kaye Chabot, Mary Lee Gavin, Karen Schirm

Meredith® Books
Editor in Chief: James D. Blume
Design Director: Matt Strelecki
Managing Editor: Gregory H. Kayko
Executive Editor, Home Decorating and Design: Denise L. Caringer

Director, Sales, Special Markets: Rita McMullen
Director, Sales, Premiums: Michael A. Peterson
Director, Sales, Retail: Tom Wierzbicki
Director, Book Marketing: Brad Elmitt
Director, Operations: George A. Susral
Director, Production: Douglas M. Johnston

Better Homes and Gardens® Magazine
Editor in Chief: Karol DeWulf Nickell
Executive Interior Design Editor: Sandra S. Soria

Meredith Publishing Group
President, Publishing Group: Stephen M. Lacy

Meredith Corporation
Chairman and Chief Executive Officer: William T. Kerr

Chairman of the Executive Committee: E. T. Meredith III

Cover Photograph: Tom McWilliam

contents

getting started

Porches and decks offer the best of both worlds: the fresh air, sights, sounds, and smells of the out-of-doors combined with many **comforts of inside.** Your porch can **welcome guests, protect family and friends** from sun and rain, and provide extra living and entertaining space. **A deck or terrace entices you** out into the garden.

A front porch is a transitional space, part public, part private. A **front porch should offer** a friendly greeting to visitors and help **set the stage for what awaits** inside. A more private side or rear porch can become an extension of your family room, with places for reading, conversation, and casual dining. Located off a bedroom, a sleeping porch creates a personal retreat for lazy afternoon naps. **With any type of porch,** the style should be relaxed and inviting. **Comfort is the key.** Who wants to while away the day in a hard chair?

A deck or balcony offers a place to sit above the dewy grass, sip a cup of morning coffee, and read the paper. **A balcony allows outside living** even in the most urban of settings. Furnishings for the deck or balcony should be flexible so it's easy to rearrange for a dinner party or an afternoon soaking up the sun.

With no protection from the elements, **deck and balcony furniture needs to be** durable and weatherproof. A market umbrella, awning, or arbor guarantees shelter from sun or rain. Bright pillows **introduce color,** and **container plants create instant walls for outdoor rooms.** Low-voltage lighting or candles in windproof hurricane chimneys extend the enjoyment into the night.

Patios and terraces, like decks and balconies, are open-air spaces. No matter if the space is a simple brick pad out back or a rooftop terrace downtown, **it can be your special place.** Choose furniture for **comfort and style,** then add plants, accessories, and garden ornaments. Keep your cool and serenity even on the hottest summer day with a gently bubbling fountain.

Foods always taste better outside. Whether it's hotdogs and lemonade with the kids or a candlelit dinner for friends, **entertaining alfresco makes any occasion special.** Fresh flowers from your garden, a crisp tablecloth, and a collection of candles transform your porch, deck, patio, or terrace into an elegant eatery.

Want to know how to make it all happen? Turn to Decorating Ideas (page 140) for ideas that you can use to create your very own space. You'll find decorating tips, project suggestions, and construction details that **you can put to use today.**

porch tours

No matter the size or location, a porch gives you the opportunity to create a special, almost magical place where life moves a little slower and the cares of the day somehow seem less pressing. Treat your porch as an outdoor room, with the same design elements used inside. Comfortable seating, lighting, accessories, and art will all help to make your porch memorable. Carefully planned furniture arrangements allow passageways while defining conversation areas.

Seating on a porch can be a pair of new rockers or your grandmother's wicker sofa and chairs, lovingly restored. Subtle lighting set on dimmers lets you adjust the mood. Add a ceiling fan to stir the breeze on still nights. Flea market finds, old garden ornaments, a section of picket fence, or brightly colored pillows signal your own personal style.

Plants belong on porches. Introduce a touch of seasonal color with a pair of container plants on either side of a small entry porch or portico. Soften a corner with ferns on a stand. Hang flower-filled baskets or classic Boston ferns between the posts. Perch pots on the railing. Let your porch blossom.

For privacy, arrange a folding screen or a hedge of tall plants. Shutter panels can hang from hooks or be permanently fastened in place to block a view, ensure privacy, or protect your porch from hot, harsh afternoon sun.

open to the breeze

Live outdoors with all the comforts of home. Let your porch express your sense of personal style.

COLOR IT UNIFIED. Turn to paint to pull together a neat, crisp decorating package. Work with a monochromatic color scheme to meld a mix of furniture shapes and styles. When mixing older pieces, prime and paint to conceal the original colors and ensure the closest possible match. For wicker, spray rather than paint for the most even coating. Be sure to select a high-quality exterior spray paint and take the time to clean each piece before painting. Practice the same preventive care to keep metal porch furniture also looking its best. If you like the timeworn look, prevent further rusting by waxing regularly with a paste wax. Use a small amount of wax, allow it to dry, and buff with a soft cloth to remove the excess. As an alternative, spray furniture with a clear sealer but test first on an inconspicuous area to make sure it's compatible with the paint finish. If you are buying new furniture, it's easy to match color by limiting your selection to one manufacturer.

■ This broad Nantucket porch, *right,* provides room for a seating group consisting of sofa, love seat, and a pair of chairs as well as a round, glass-topped dining table and chairs. A window box, planted with summer flowers, brings the colors of the garden deep into the porch at a pleasing height.

■ The generous scale of the porch, *opposite,* allows space for a metal table and chairs that bring to mind a turn-of-the-20th-century ice cream parlor or the bentwood furniture of Thonet. The slight weathering and rusting add to the carefree look. Flower baskets add a finishing touch.

SHOWCASE PLANTS. Make an outdoor space truly a garden room by encouraging plants to grow everywhere. Rotate containers for seasonal color. Include plenty of places for plants in and around your outdoor room. If your outdoor room opens to a large garden or lawn, add extra seating away from the house to create a focal point and an attractive garden destination.

■ For this arbored terrace, *above,* gaps in the stone around the base of each post create small planting beds for climbing vines. As an alternative, pots could be placed

at the base of each post. In addition to the vine-covered arbor, a simple trellis leads a trail of green up the side of the house The weathered teak chairs and table seem to disappear among the vine-covered posts. The small, round grille set in the end of the stone wall conceals a low-voltage bulb that lights the garden path.

■ A low stone wall, *right,* elevates a row of pots. More flowers fill the raised planter boxes set in front of the stone wall. Simple boxes are easy to make from pressure-treated boards nailed together with galvanized nails, or better yet, fastened with galvanized or stainless wood screws. If treated wood has not been kiln-dried after treatment, it should be allowed to weather for a few weeks before painting. The Adirondack chairs, painted bright white, anchor the view and add extra seating on mild days.

■ Weathered, rustic birdhouses, *below,* complement the overall color scheme. Brightly colored accessories could seem out of character in this New England setting. Instead, the simplicity of the little houses recalls the charm of seaside summer cottages.

CONSIDER THE SCALE.

CONSIDER THE SCALE. On a small porch, choose furniture and accessories that won't overpower the scale. Select a wicker or twig love seat or settee instead of a full-size sofa or glider, for example.

■ Although this porch, *opposite,* is limited in size, it includes all the basics of a sitting area: comfortable seating for four. Two open white twig chairs and a white wicker settee impart a light, airy look. For flexibility, all the furniture is lightweight enough to be rearranged without fuss. Flowering plants in small terra-cotta pots rotate between porch and garden. Massing them adds impact.

■ Incorporating a few key accessories makes a porch seem complete, but not cluttered, *above.* The vase and the birdhouse are examples of collectibles that work well in a variety of locations. Pillows offer another way to add color and character without making the porch visually heavy. Here the pillow fabrics repeat the botanical theme of the plant-filled porch.

■ Peeling paint and edges softened with decades of use, *top right,* impart a timeless quality to porch furniture that can't be purchased with new pieces. Different styles of furniture that are all the same color give a more unified, organized look to a smaller porch.

■ A table for porch use must be able to withstand high humidity and heavy usage. This tile top, *lower right,* offers a practical and lively solution. The soft colors of the mosaic tile and the open steel base lighten the look of the piece. Tile-topped tables are available in a variety of sizes, shapes, and patterns and are also do-it-yourself projects that can be custom-sized.

ADD TOUCHES OF HOME. The more comfortable and inviting you make your porch, the more your family and friends use it. Choose furniture based on how comfortable it is for sitting and lounging, not just on how it looks. Add plush cushions and plenty of pillows. Always include a place to prop your feet and a spot to rest a cold drink.

▒ The stuccoed end wall, pierced by a semicircular lunette window, assures privacy on this second-floor piazza in Charleston, South Carolina, *opposite.* In this historic city noted for its porches—called piazzas—the spaces become true outdoor living rooms furnished with sofas, tables, and lamps. Here a grouping of wicker invites the visitor to sit in the shade and relax. New wicker is available in a range of colors, from white to traditional Charleston green, an almost black-green. Older wicker pieces, which are increasingly difficult to find, especially in matched sets, can be spray-painted to a desired shade.

▒ As with any sitting room, a porch needs places to hold drinks or books between chapters. The end table, *below,* is small enough to tuck into a corner, yet large enough to be useful. Inspired by an olive-oil jar, the rustic, French-style lamp casts a soft glow over after-dinner conversation and extends reading hours into the night. Floor lamps offer another option for serious nighttime readers. Accent pillows, all in soft floral prints, complement the ferns and flowers of the lush piazza setting.

ACCESSORIES SET THE MOOD. The furnishings you choose set the mood for your porch. Simple, even inexpensive, furnishings that fit the space and your family's lifestyle are better than overpriced, pretentious pieces. If you want your porch to evoke the ambience of a farmhouse in the South of France or the Italian hill country, choose tables and chairs that look as though they received years of use and decades of exposure to the warm sun and rain. Limit accessories to fresh flowers, handmade pottery, baskets, and found objects.

■ Elegantly simple, this outdoor dining area, *opposite,* suggests the sunny colors and rustic farm tables of southern Europe. Tie-on cushions in an off-white cotton add comfort to the rush-bottom, ladder-back chairs. For a unified look, the chairs are painted the same pale peach as the stucco walls. The table was stripped of its paint finish and left to weather naturally for a mellow look.

■ Favorite objects introduce personal touches to porch decorating. The baker's rack, *left,* provides a spot to display plants, shells, a glazed olive oil jar, and other favorites. Similar racks are available as vintage or reproduction pieces. Baskets are used alone and as textural containers for green plants. Stacked baskets elevate the ivy. An individual tile supported on a plate stand adds a spot of color to the setting. A starfish and seashell allude to the nearby Atlantic.

MIX IN METAL. Decorate with a variety of materials for both furnishings and accessories that impart an eclectic look to your outdoor space. An old iron garden gate or section of railing adds an attractive accent, often at an affordable price. Tuck a small metal fern stand into a

corner where a wood piece would seem too bulky. When shopping for a metal table, pay particular attention to the base. Is it sturdy? Does it wobble? Replace a damaged top with new glass, stone, or even painted plywood for a contemporary look.

▓ The shapely metal chairs, *above,* recall Parisian cafe chairs. Both light in weight and visually open, the chairs give surprising comfort when fitted with tie-on cushions. Folding chairs, such as vintage wood or reproduction bamboo styles, add extra seating for special occasions. The diamond-frame window is instant art.

▓ Simply leaning a decorative piece of ironwork on the porch railing, *left,* stops the eye and effectively screens the view. On old metalwork, rust or layers of paint only strengthen charm. Combining metal chairs and a table base with a glass top keeps the look light and clean. Painted white to blend with the walls and piled with pillows, this porch swing offers a comfortable and fun substitute for a conventional sofa. While vintage swings are occasionally available at antique shops, new ones are reasonably priced at home center stores and some casual furniture dealers. To replicate the look of a tile floor, the porch is hand-painted in black and white squares set on the diagonal. Painted floors can be sealed with polyurethane or allowed to wear naturally.

ENRICHING THE STYLE. If you are planning a porch remodeling or addition, strive to make it compatible with your existing house style. Look through architectural history books or guides for ideas of porches that would meld with your house and neighborhood. Repeat a key style feature such as an arch or window style to unify old and new.

■ For the porch addition, *right,* to a Tudor-style house in Dallas, Texas, the design repeats the distinctive four-centered arches of the home's existing windows for the openings and for the fireplace above. The addition also duplicates many of the materials used on the existing interior and exterior to guarantee the porch a character in keeping with the original house. The porch is a true year-round room with the inclusion of the fireplace with raised hearth. In warmer weather, the hearth provides a spot to display a container plant. An old cast-iron grating hangs above the mantel, flanked with sconces. The availability of direct-vented and zero-clearance prefabricated fireplaces makes it easier to add a fireplace to a new or existing porch. However, local code restrictions vary.

■ Matching materials tie the new porch to the older Tudor house. When matching isn't possible, a slight offset in a wall helps the visual transition. Brick walls and flagstone floors, *opposite,* replicate materials used in the original house. The stone floor also makes a rugged, low-maintenance surface, important for an outdoor room that gets heavy use. The sea-grass sofa, chaise, and chair fit the scale of the large space. Although light in color, the pieces have the substantial look the room demands. Easy-care fabrics and washable slipcovers keep the cushions and pillows looking good. The Lone Star wall inset suits the setting.

art of the porch

Consider your porch a fresh-air gallery for art—and artful accessories—that you change with your mood.

CREATE AN ART-FILLED RETREAT. Whether you paint or simply collect and appreciate, prowl antique shops, garage sales, and salvage yards for accessories. Search for ordinary, everyday objects that you can put to new uses. Use your imagination and collect what appeals to you.

■ With easel and paint at the ready, this porch, *above,* becomes a studio as well as a place for entertaining family and friends. There's a swing for sitting, a simple board bench that does double-duty as a coffee table and extra seating, and a table for serving. A galvanized bucket and a watering can display cut flowers. Once part of a stairway, a pair of newel posts gains a second life as sculptures that frames the old-fashioned swing.

■ With a little imagination, an arrangement of ordinary things transforms into a three-dimensional still life, *opposite*. Fruits, vegetables, flowers, found objects, and flea market finds contribute their own beauty to this porch. A simple painted pine table holds a colorful spread of edible art while a scale weighs a stack of old books. On the wall, an ornately framed reproduction balances the charming and artful vignette.

SIMPLE AND NATURAL. Let the art for your porch come from nature. Flowers and plants accent and enrich a fresh-air space with their ever-changing colors and textures. Found objects from nature—shells, rocks, driftwood, old birds' nests, or pinecones— share interesting forms and shapes. Fresh fruit and vegetables from the grocery or garden become art you can eat. Group similar items in a tray, bowl, or basket for extra impact. Remember that everything doesn't have to be at eye level. Place art on or near the floor to fill an empty corner. Extend paintings or prints up a wall to emphasize a tall ceiling. Set a piece in an unexpected place. Enjoy the results.

An apple-filled basket, *above,* forms an edible centerpiece on this coffee table. The cluster of inexpensive flowerpots filled with blooming plants accents a wicker table set between a pair of rockers. Wiping the terra-cotta pots with white paint helps them blend with the porch and its furnishings. A flowering vine wraps artfully around a metal topiary frame to form a living sculpture. Twig-style frames border the matted flower prints.

Accents from the garden and the sea grace this sunlight-dappled porch, *opposite.* Starfish fill the shelf of a wicker serving bar. Cut flowers fresh from the garden and simply displayed in a glass pitcher transform into a still life. A colorfully framed old photograph leans casually against the porch rail. To unify this collection of antique wicker, all the pieces are spray-painted a soft white, and floral print pillows and cushions are added.

ADD SOMETHING OLD. Pieces of the past evoke a timeless quality for a porch or any space. They also offer a way to showcase interests in collecting, gardening, bird-watching, fishing, or other pursuits. Check out antique stores, flea markets, and garage and tag sales. Stores specializing in architectural salvage are a good source for old doors, shutters, brackets, and light fixtures that provide rustic and delightfully aged backdrops for your collectibles.

■ A wall-mounted rack displays potted plants and a pair of lighthouse models, *opposite upper left*. On the table below, matching plants and lanterns flank a tin-roofed birdhouse, creating a symmetrically balanced arrangement. Considered more formal than asymmetrical, symmetrical balance uses items placed the same distance from the centerline for order.

■ An ornately carved wood bracket rests atop a porch railing, *left*. Just below, three old shutter panels hinged together create a screen to fill the corner. The metal pedestal-base table takes on a look far different from its restaurant roots when covered with an antique tablecloth. Suspending the chandelier from an exposed beam refines the setting with a touch of elegance.

■ Old doesn't have to mean that old. On this porch, *above,* a pair of butterfly chairs from the 1950s combines with a variety of other furniture and accessories for an eclectic look. Sap buckets add a touch of color next to the chair. A bait shop sign as well as two fish-shaped racks decorate the beaded-board wall for a fishing theme. In the far corner, an old wood ladder and a door with its peeling paint balance as vertical accents. Several whimsical figures share the tabletop with plants, clay lanterns, potted plants, and books. The simple board bench doubles as a coffee table. Old benches sometimes can be hard to find, but crafting one is an easy afternoon project. The only tools needed are a handsaw and a hammer.

well-furnished porch

To make your porch a true outdoor room, incorporate the comforts of home, including tables and pillows.

■ The furniture arrangement on the large front porch, *left,* echoes the floor plan inside. The center of the porch is clear of furniture, defining a center hall from the steps to the front door. A three-cushion wicker sofa anchors the conversation group, just as one would for the living room inside. Two comfortable armchairs complete the grouping. A large planter box and a section of shutter stop the eye at the edge of the inviting and colorfully decorated porch.

■ An armless chair, *opposite,* tucks inconspicuously into a corner, yet pulls out when extra seating is needed. A simple ladder-back chair with a cane seat similar to this one can be found at many antique stores. The joints should be tight and the seat and back secure. A tie-on cushion or pillow adds comfort and color.

■ A small square table, *below,* makes a versatile porch piece for games, casual dining, or as a buffet. A 32-inch square or 36-inch-diameter round table seats four comfortably for brunch or bridge. The height should be about 29 inches with at least 2 feet of clearance from the bottom of the apron to the floor.

LIVING ON THE PORCH. If your porch is large, arrange two groups of seating, with each no more than 12 feet square, which is a size that encourages conversation. Too large an area seems spread out and makes it difficult to hear what's being said. A too-small grouping feels crowded. Allow plenty of room for circulation so guests can go from outside to inside without climbing over furniture. At a minimum, allow 3 feet between furniture for the path from the steps to the front door.

■ Plants and accessories relax and soften an outdoor room. This end of a large porch, *left,* features a swing instead of a sofa. A blanket chest serves as a coffee table while a decoratively painted bench displays collectibles.

COOL AND INVITING. The color scheme you choose for your porch inspires the mood for the entire space. If the body and trim colors of the house can't be changed, the color choices on the porch will be limited to furniture, accessories, and perhaps the porch floor and ceiling. Because the porch will be visible from both the outside and inside, consider it in context of what you see from inside the house and from the street or lawn.

The white of the exterior trim carries through onto the porch and even inside where it is used as trim color, *left*. Because the body of the house is a deep red, the white-on-white color scheme of the porch provides a soothing contrast. Crisp white furniture, trim, and linens cool down the barn-red siding. Even the caned oak porch rockers and bench are painted white to strengthen the summery mood. Touches of color are added or changed merely by swapping blooming plants or by moving cushions and pillows. Accessories, such as the bright red birdhouse, offer another way to include color. While the old-fashioned flower cart is painted white, it's filled with colorful blooming begonias.

Even this child's folding chair, *above,* reinforces the white-on-white scheme. Seating just their size is always appreciated by children, but pieces should be sturdy and free of splinters and sharp edges. Likewise, child-size folding chairs should be tested to make sure they won't collapse or pinch little fingers. The small glass and metal table repurposes as a generously sized plant stand.

TOUCHED WITH GREEN. Because the color is everywhere in nature, green is an excellent way to bring a feel of the forest, fields, and garden onto a porch. Plants are an obvious choice, sharing soothing colors, fragrant smells, and a wide variety of textures. Paint offers a quick and relatively easy way to introduce a touch of green to the porch floor, shutters, or trim. The fabrics and accessories you choose add green and other nature-inspired tones. Let nearby plants be your guide when selecting the greens you plan to use. Foliage colors range from dark to pale.

■ Green cools this porch, *above,* pulling the outside in. The green floor, fern basket, and shutters suggest touches of nature on the white porch. Even the chains supporting the rocker are covered in matching fabric. The green floor absorbs light, reducing glare. It does absorb heat, making a sun-drenched area hot for bare feet.

■ Matching cushions unify the antique wicker, *opposite.* Shutters impart a touch of green and frame openings. If only decorative, each shutter should be about half the width of the window so the shutter looks as if it could close completely.

■ Wall-mounted containers, such as this ornate example, *above left,* are a good way to add both height and a touch of color to the wall. If necessary, a container can be painted or glazed to match the porch. Plants do best if suited to the light level and filled in with sphagnum moss for a finished look. For a more delicate look, new or vintage hall-hung vases, including those handblown in the style of Italian glass, can be filled with seasonal garden flowers. Vintage pottery wall vases are finds at flea markets and antique fairs.

■ Even the smallest accessories carry through the color scheme. Three green bud vases filled with zinnias from the garden introduce a colorful accent to a tabletop display, *above*. An old wire basket corrals a collection of seashells. When antique examples of prized wire baskets are hard to find, import stores offer attractive reproductions that work in a variety of decors. The antique bell imparts another element of age to the setting.

wicker&rockers

Encourage your guests to linger with the classic combination of summery wicker and sturdy rockers.

SIT A SPELL. Having plenty of places to sit makes a porch even more enjoyable. Choose each piece for comfort and appearance. If you can't find a matching set, mix a variety of pieces. Use color to unify by spray-painting everything the same shade. Tie the scheme together with cushions and pillows in matching or coordinated fabrics. Check to see if old wicker is real wicker or more fragile wrapped paper, which doesn't hold up as well on a porch. Look for wood rockers with turned-down edges on the seat front for maximum comfort. Check the balance; some rockers feel as though they will topple over if you lean back.

■ The wood settee and wicker rocker, *opposite above,* work together, courtesy of white paint. The settee is a central European piece, furniture that is becoming easier to find. With a well-worn, pale blue finish, the board coffee table is a country-style find at flea markets.

■ A pair of dark green rockers and two wicker armchairs provide seating on this traditional front porch, *opposite below.* The wicker ottoman does double duty as a coffee table. A matching plaid fabric on the three wicker pieces contains a dark green stripe to coordinate with the two rockers. Plump throw pillows also help to tie the seating together.

■ Here everybody can be on the move in a pair of rockers and a wicker swing, *below.* The fabric chosen for the pillows and cushions melds together the sitting group and sets the tone for the entire space. Like blue-and-white china, blue-and-white fabric ensures a classic look. Even though the patterns on these prints vary from stripes to florals to plaids, the colors are close enough to unify the setting. The cool, restful blues create a good backdrop for the red accents of the napkin and red geraniums. The small wicker table covered with the vintage-style cloth measures about 29 inches—standard dining height.

WRAPPED BY PORCHES.

If you are lucky enough to have an L-shape porch or front and back porches, take advantage of morning and afternoon exposures. You'll find sunny and shady places throughout the day as you follow the sun. If sun control is an issue, install roll-down canvas or bamboo shades.

Three antique rush-bottom rockers, *right,* occupy one end of the long side porch. The dark, almost black-green chosen for the chairs and other pieces is known as Charleston green. Next to the rocker, an old box serves as an end table. A column salvaged from a house being torn down finds a new life as a tall plant stand. If an old column can't be found, new ones are available at home centers and building supply stores to paint or stain. In the foreground, a five-board bench elevates a pot and conch shell.

On this front porch, *left,* a small seating area welcomes guests. Although different in style and color from the pair of benches on the side porch, this white-painted bench repeats the massing and the striped fabric cushion. The glass-topped, parsons-style coffee table imparts a sleek, contemporary contrast to the wicker chair. A round skirted table works for serving and display space at the end of the bench. Inexpensive plywood tops and bases are available in a variety of sizes. Or a round top can be added to an existing table or a low chest before skirting.

At the other end of the porch, *above,* a pair of wood benches from an old lodge anchors two seating groupings separated by a skirted table. Each grouping has its own coffee table and complement of chairs. Sisal area rugs define the two spaces. For a small gathering, one bench and two chairs are sufficient. For a larger party, guests can spread out to form two separate conversation areas or pull in extra chairs to make a single large one. The far coffee table was originally a dining table; the legs were cut down to coffee table height, approximately 18 inches.

SCHEMING ABOUT COLOR. As these three examples show, you can choose from a variety of options when selecting a porch color scheme. The exterior colors of the house certainly may be a factor, as could be nearby houses. The colors used inside may flow outside, especially from rooms adjoining the porch. The most important consideration is the mood you wish to set. White-painted wicker and soft pastels inspire calm; brighter colors set a lively, active tone. For a color palette that can be changed or updated easily, stay with a basic color such as white or dark green for larger pieces, then introduce color with pillows or other accessories that can be easily swapped.

■ For a relaxed, slightly contemporary look, this porch and deck, *above,* combine muted colors ranging from off-white to light khaki. The result is soft and serene. Accessories such as pillows, cushions, and planter boxes reinforce the same neutral range. Glass containers contribute shape.

■ In keeping with the colorful Victorian exterior of this 1884 house, the porch, *above,* features rich hues on all the trim as well as the furnishings. Purple accents on the porch railing and posts are echoed on the spindle-turned rockers and on the area rug. The small twig table was popular a century ago and is still available. The pale blue ceiling is an historic tradition, reputed to keep away flying insects.

■ From the wicker swing and chair to the lush fern, this generously scaled porch, *left,* recalls the romantic fresh-air spaces of the Victorian era. Cushions and pillows in soft pastels create an easy, convivial feeling in the space. The rag rug helps tie together the small seating area. A patchwork quilt draped over the painted country rocker contributes a welcome and warming addition on a cool night. The campaign-style table adds another 19th-century accent to the inviting scene. Large ferns elevated to seated eye level provide a sense of privacy and enclosure.

private retreats

A secluded location, enhanced if necessary by airy draperies or sheers, creates a soul-soothing getaway.

OUTDOOR ESCAPES. With thoughtful design and siting, a porch is a private place to get away from the pressures of the world. Usually a rear or side porch offers the best choices. Located far from the noises of the street and the eyes of passersby, such a porch often achieves privacy with little effort. A front porch, however, if not in a quiet location well back from the street, requires screening to block views from the outside. Louvered shutters, roll-down blinds, curtains, or even strategically placed plants accomplish the job. A porch with the floor located at least 5 feet above the ground feels more private than a lower one.

■ Located at the rear, this porch, *left,* is screened by two sides of the house. The garage offers additional screening. To-the-floor draperies ensure a sense of enclosure. A sofa and chair, slipcovered in white, contribute a comfortable feel to the space. Slipcovering updates existing furniture and allows easy cleaning, important on a porch. The upholstered pieces are set well back on the porch to protect them from blowing rain. A cut-down dining table, the coffee table takes on new life with a coat of white paint. In the background, a chaise lounge awaits an afternoon napper. Ficus trees in wicker baskets bring in the garden.

■ A brick arcade, *opposite below,* encloses this ground-level porch. The setting, a large, wooded lot, assures a measure of privacy. Wide brick piers provide more screening for the porch than would narrow wood posts. Fern-filled baskets also help define and screen the porch. This low-maintenance floor is concrete, scored on the diagonal and accented with square tile insets. The rustic table features a log base.

■ Cast stone, a popular option for the garden, comes onto the porch. This stone piece, *below,* serves as an end table and a buffet. Because cast stone is heavy, the floor may have to be reinforced. Cast stone can be stained with a thin wash of paint for an aged look or coated with buttermilk and left outside to develop a patina. The ornamental metal astrolabe, a device once used for determining the position of the stars, shares tabletop display with a miniature greenhouse and potted herbs.

DRAPED IN STYLE. Window treatments screen as effectively outside as inside. Choose a fabric that resists mildew and holds up well to repeated washings. A fabric designed specifically for outdoor use is the safest choice, but color and pattern choices are somewhat limited. Cotton duck, available in a variety of weights, is a traditional option. Depending on the effect you want, choose a gauzy fabric to blow in the breeze or a heavier one for a tailored look. Standard indoor hardware can be used in a protected location, but for long-term service, choose materials such as solid brass, bronze, or stainless steel that don't rust or corrode.

■ Set behind a brick arcade, this series of interconnected outdoor spaces, *opposite above,* serves a row of ground-level rooms, giving each interior room its own outdoor space. For privacy, each of the outdoor rooms can be closed off by drawing the fabric panels. Brass rods, mounted to the ceiling, support the panels. A pair of full-size daybeds allow for afternoon naps. A clean, contemporary circular dining table, set between the two daybeds, is large enough for a meal or a game of cards. The folding chairs are teak, a tropical wood that stands up well outdoors even without a finish.

■ Stacked stone forms a rustic table that contrasts with the sleek, tailored metal daybed, *opposite below.* The use of stone also echoes the flagstone floor in the space. Flat, irregularly shaped stone can be found in the garden section of many home center stores.

■ Green-and-white stripe fabric panels, gathered on rods, frame the corners of this porch, *above.* Tiebacks of the same fabric keep the panels in place in the wind. For a full look, the fabric panel should be about twice the width of the rod. The semicircular dormer brings additional light into the high-ceiling porch.

KEEPING OUT THE SUN. For a porch that faces west, blocking the hot afternoon sun with curtains, draperies, shades, or blinds is as crucial as providing privacy. For maximum screening, use a heavy fabric, preferably in a dark color. To filter the light, opt for a thin, white fabric. Draperies or curtains on rings or traverse rods close or open as needed. Roll-down shades work best if the length and weight are not excessive. Blinds allow the greatest degree of sun control because they can be adjusted from opened to closed or raised completely. Louvered shutters offer another alternative but block much of the view.

Billowing white draperies enrich the nautical theme of this porch, *opposite*. A system of rods and rings mounted near the ceiling lets the porch be closed off or opened up easily. The lightweight fabric filters the sunlight, reducing glare and heat, but allows considerable light. The eclectic mix of furnishings includes a pair of French Colonial armchairs painted red, and a combination coffee table-chessboard. The curved stool in the left corner is a Chinese piece; the large model sailboat is known as a pond yacht. Older ones as well as reproductions can be found in antique shops.

Roll-up canvas shades between the columns ensure easy sun control on this waterfront porch, *above*. The shades have individual panels that can be raised or lowered by cords. A cleat, fastened to one of the columns at a convenient height, allows the cords to be tied as needed. The canvas is a caramel color to complement the cream trim and brown rocker.

SOUTHWESTERN TOUCHES. The distinctive style of the American Southwest lends itself to outdoor living. Hallmarks of the style include sturdy, often rough-hewn furnishings, earthy colors, and metal accents. As the border nearby, the influences of Mexican art and architecture are often seen.

▓ With posts and railings made from logs, this porch, *above*, takes on a decided rustic look. The swing is a variation on the familiar Adirondack chair. Cowboy collectibles, such as this Hopalong Cassidy wastebasket and colorful boots, complete the effect. Hanging the swing high and close to the railing gives the best view of the river valley below.

▓ A pierced-tin light fixture and a brightly decorated vase show the Mexican touches on this covered deck, *above right*. Small area rugs below the steel-frame table impart elegance. Fabric cushions on the chairs repeat the soft red of the trim.

▓ White wicker introduces an elegant touch to the small porch of this log house, *right*. When space is tight, a pair of comfortable armchairs and a small dining table allow maximum flexibility for seating and dining. When needed, the table can be pulled out and two folding chairs added.

▓ Finished and refined, this screen porch, *opposite*, is a true outdoor room. The stuccoed walls that mimic adobe and the ceiling of peeled logs recall the construction methods once popular in the desert Southwest. The chair is Mission style.

screen

If you plan to spend any time at all on a porch, consider screening it. While the flickering glow of fireflies can be charming, the humming (and biting) of mosquitoes is anything but. Insect screening not only makes a porch more usable, but it also provides a sense of enclosure. By day, the screen helps filter light and reduce glare. At night, light shining on the screen turns it into a sheltering wall. With the insects out of the way, a screen porch transforms into an extra dining room. When space is at a premium, a folding table and a pair of chairs evoke the feeling of a Parisian cafe, yet can slip away into a nearby closet.

If you have the space, a permanent dining table on the porch will make outdoor meals easier and more frequent, as well as provide a work surface for school projects. For reading, add at least one comfortable chair and ottoman. A sofa can double as a daybed. Pile it with pillows for an added feeling of luxury. Provide a coffee table large enough to hold the Sunday paper and the breakfast bagels. Lamps rated for outdoor use extend reading time after sundown. Let your own taste dictate the porch's style. Tie it back to the rest of the house or let it go in another direction. Create the look of a rustic mountain cabin or a seaside retreat. Fill your screened porch with ferns and wicker to evoke a Victorian feel. Just keep it easy, relaxed, and personal.

screenporches

Protected from sun, rain, and insects, a screen porch is often the favorite room in the house.

SOFT COLORS AT THE SEASIDE. Re-create the relaxed charm of a Florida cottage by blending colors and finishes that emulate the gentle wear of sun and rain. For a muted color scheme to blend harmoniously, restrict all the tones—furniture, surfaces, art, and accessories—to subtle shades. Consider that the addition of a single bright, saturated item can upset the desired effect. Note that value—the lightness or darkness of a color—is important. Even reds and blues can be tinted with white to reduce their intensities, giving the soft pastel effect associated with the well-worn seaside summer houses.

■ An old porch glider, *above right,* relaxes the setting with the gentle rocking movement of a swing without the chains. This metal example was given a fresh coat of paint and a striped cushion. Similar pieces are available from yard or tag sales and thrift stores; reproductions are also on the market. Six metal chairs, tied with cotton ticking

cushions, cluster around an old farm table. Such sturdy tables work well for casual meals, buffet service, and rainy-day activities. The edging of the bound sisal rug matches the terra-cotta shade. Hung on the wall, a pair of natural baskets transforms into instant art.

■ With a picket fence backboard, this small, simple table, *opposite below,* works as the focal point for an inviting porch scene. If a table of similar size can't be found, pickets are available at many lumber yards and home centers. However, the selection of shapes may be limited. The dough bowl on the shelf below is carved wood. Sold in a variety of shapes and sizes, antique bowls are handy for serving and for display. Although this is a new house, the lap siding imbues the porch with the pleasantly added-on look of older beach cottages.

■ A galvanized storage bin, *left,* proves just the right height for a bar. Similar industrial items are prized finds at salvage yards. As an alternative, an old two-drawer office file cabinet can be spray-painted to serve as a bar or end table. Drawers add convenient storage for magazines, napkins, or other accessories. For stand-up serving, the piece should be between table height, about 29 inches, and kitchen counter height, 36 inches. If necessary, short legs or casters can be added to a piece for extra height.

A PORCH FULL OF WICKER. For a traditional screen porch that recalls summers of long ago, decorate with romantic white wicker. With both old and new pieces widely available in white, you can mix wicker ages and styles to furnish your porch. Matching sets of antique wicker can be hard to find and often command a premium price, but individual pieces or pairs of chairs are easier to acquire. Be sure to check the entire piece, even underneath, for damage. Before buying any chair or sofa, sit on it. Some pieces of wicker can be uncomfortable; that's not what you want on your porch.

■ A variety of wicker pieces creates a comfortable ensemble, *above*. No two pieces are exactly alike, yet the effect is unified by the classic porch styles. A white cotton area rug further ties together the grouping. The chains supporting the rocker are covered with fabric tubes sewn from the same pale green material used for some of the cushions and pillows. Oversize bows complete the romantic effect. A wall-mounted hook holds a flower-filled hanging basket for all to see. For sun control, white matchstick blinds roll down inside; on the exterior, heavier canvas shades provide extra weather protection.

Many different accessory pieces still can be found in antique shops, including tables, plant stands, and even lights. Here a wicker end table ornately supports an arrangement of fresh flowers, *top right.*

Pillows and cushions, *right,* offer an easy, changeable way to introduce color. For comfort, the bottom cushion is thick enough to prevent the front edge of the chair from digging into the back of the leg. Down or fiberfill cushions compress with use. Foam-filled cushions retain their original shape, but some people find them hard and uncomfortable.

COLOR IT GREEN. For a cool take on tradition, choose deep green for painted wicker porch furniture. Deep forest shades look and feel soothing on hot days and pair with wood-tone furnishings and natural sisal rugs. The green reflects less light than white, reducing glare, an important consideration if you like to read on the porch. Although harder to find than white, old pieces are available for the diligent shopper. As an alternative, new or secondhand white wicker can be spray-painted in your color choice.

■ Plenty of cushions and pillows in light-colored floral and striped fabrics contrast with the dark green of the wicker porch furniture, *above*. The coffee table with drawer adds handy concealed storage. A skylight in the porch ceiling brings in extra natural light. Skylights help balance light levels on a deep porch and increase natural light in an interior room shaded by a porch. Unless the skylight is shaded by trees, as here, the light could be too bright. A striped awning shades outside for additional sun control.

■ The dark green floor works with the green of the wicker for a restful effect on this screen porch, *above*. The long, narrow table can be used as shown, with a pair of simple benches for casual dining. For buffet serving, the table can be pushed against the wall and the benches placed along the screened side of the porch for extra seating. A pair of large star-motif brackets decorates the wall.

■ Accessories emphasize the green theme of this sitting porch, *left*. The green-and-white stripe fabric on the sofa, the lampshade, and the plants all contribute. Because there are variations in shades of green used for wicker, matching everything proves to be a challenge. Here all the pieces are new wicker from the same manufacturer so they match. When working with old wicker, often the only option for a perfect match is to repaint everything the same paint shade. Spray-painting is easy and effective.

RAISE THE ROOF. Expand the spacious feeling of a screen porch by going up, not out. A high ceiling makes any room seem more open. For a porch, a higher ceiling has the extra effect of allowing warm air to rise, making the space cooler in summer. A high ceiling also brings more light into the room and into the interior of the house. Glass-filled pediments, dormers, clerestory windows, and cupolas can introduce light high up in the room. Although raising the ceiling of an existing porch is a major undertaking, increasing the ceiling height of a new porch may add little to the construction costs. Most often, the limiting factor is how the porch roof ties into the rest of the house. Choose a ceiling material and finish—natural wood, stained, or painted—compatible with your home style.

■ The high, arched roof of this porch addition, *opposite,* turns it into a dramatic space that recalls a hunting lodge or perhaps an aircraft hanger. The semicircular glass in the end wall welcomes more light and offers views up to the treetops. The exposed beams and roof decking display their interesting structure. Furnishings include a pair of unusual upholstered wicker armchairs.

■ Rather than a simple door, a pair of French doors with sidelights and transoms, *left,* opens from the interior of the house to the porch. The architectural glass doors allow the interior room to borrow light from the porch.

■ Even a small space such as the breakfast area, *above,* benefits from a raised ceiling. Because privacy isn't an issue, openings are as large as possible without window treatments. The metal chairs and glass-top table let the view star.

■ Hexagonal tile creates a free-flowing pattern on this screened porch, *left.* Worn paint on the furniture, old advertising signs, and simple accessories combine to produce a relaxed country feel. The aged look is achieved easily on a new piece by layering on several colors, then sanding through in spots to duplicate normal wear.

■ For a unique, yet durable floor, *right,* the standard terra-cotta tiles were broken into randomly shaped pieces. The pieces were then laid using conventional thin-set mortar and grouted. Fitted jigsaw-puzzle style, the arrangement maximizes the grout lines. The corner fireplace is an inexpensive, portable chimenea from Mexico with a stovepipe added. Red oxide primer on the stovepipe matches the color of the clay. Homeowners should check local building codes before adding any type of fireplace or wood-burning stove to a porch.

■ The shades of the clear-finished wood siding and a leather and wood chair, *below,* complement the warm browns of the terra-cotta tile floor. The weathered paint on the old louvered door enhances the rustic charm of the space. Behind the door is a storage closet, useful for folding chairs.

TILED TO LAST. Remember that your porch floor must be tough to withstand wear and weather. One option is a durable tile floor. Properly installed, it can hold up to years of use. As with any type of tilework, surface preparation is important. The best base for a tile floor is a concrete slab which provides a rigid substrate that won't flex or shift, cracking the tile. A sturdy wood floor can be tiled, but first a layer of cement backer board should be screwed in place in a thin bed of mortar. Choose the tile with longevity in mind. Because trendy colors go out of style, stay with basic tile colors and patterns that have withstood time and taste changes.

THINK NATURAL AND NEUTRAL. Create a restful color scheme with
varied textures of natural materials. For an easy start, paint surfaces off-white
and work in lots of tans and khakis. Remember that because there is no real
color, the textures give the room character and substance. Feel free to mix
styles, shapes, and shades from sleeker rattan and metal pieces to old-
fashioned wicker to country oak rockers; their tones are in the natural range.

▓ Rattan and wicker, new and old, harmonize in this neutral environment,
left. Soft colors on the walls and trim are complemented by the large natural
sisal rug spread across the pine porch floor. A simple potting table, worn with
time, displays pots in a variety of containers; below, a large wood basket
holds a summery fern. The window treatments are rectangular panels of
gauzy fabric, each measuring about 12 inches wider than the opening.
Ends of each panel tie to a bamboo rod mounted to the casing with closet
rod brackets. Frosted glass ceramic wall vases line porch columns.

▓ A concrete birdbath finds a new use inside with a glass top added to
become an occasional table, *above left.* Another option is as a magazine
holder. Concrete can be painted with diluted paint for a color-washed effect.
The natural wood of the old Mississippi porch rocker reinforces the neutral
theme. A butterfly net leans against the wall, awaiting the next chase.

▓ Tucked below the glass, *above right,* colorful seed packets and a collection
of antique gardening tools rest on a bed of polished river rock. Clear plastic
pads, half an inch in diameter, can shim a glass top on uneven pieces.

AWASH IN LIGHT. Start your porch decorating project with a bare room, removing furnishings and stripping the space down to the essentials you want to keep. Then think about what you like and want to keep and what you can do to make the space more enjoyable. When your budget is limited, don't be timid. Pick a theme and carry it through all the way. Paint and pillows are inexpensive, especially as part of a do-it-yourself facelift. For finishing touches, adapt items to new uses: Turn jars into table bases, or use plants or architectural salvage for art.

▓ Three plump pillows soften the simple wood-slat swing, *right*. More pillows, stacked on the floor, provide extra seating.

The area rug is of woven grass, available from import stores. At the fixed-screened windows, sheer curtain panels hang on tension rods placed above eye level to maximize privacy and light. These were a do-it-yourself project, but ready-made cafe curtains offer another alternative. Below the assembled glass table, with import store jars for bases, a wire basket corrals a collection of seashells. Plants in a variety of containers lend a tropical air.

▓ Three delicately colored glass candle holders dangle from metal rods found at a garden shop, *below*. For stability, the tall galvanized bucket is filled with sand. Ceramic jars or concrete urns offer substitutes for the glass jars.

PLACES FOR PLANTS. Like people, plants enjoy being out on the porch. The fresh air, filtered sunlight, and a little care will encourage houseplants to blossom and bloom. Use plants like art or any other accessory to brighten or heighten a corner, fill an empty wall, or soften a hard edge. Choose containers that enhance your look: terra-cotta pots for a simple ambience or more ornate china cachepots for a formal effect. Remember that potted plants require frequent watering, so purchase containers that won't leak. To be safe, use a plastic pot and saucer inside a larger pot. Hide the plastic with sphagnum moss from a nursery or plant store.

■ A variety of plant shapes and sizes enriches this screen porch, *left*. A pair of ficus fills a corner with green even when the trees outside have dropped their leaves for the winter. An ornate baker's rack set against the wall displays small container plants. The large lower shelf can also be used for buffet service. Originally designed to showcase breads and pastries, baker's racks have been revived by a number of furniture manufacturers for use in the home. The intricate semicircular fragment above the sofa is half of a molded foam ceiling medallion, available in the lighting sections of most home centers and some discount stores.

■ For proper fit, the window box measures the width of the window, *above*. A window box used inside should be sealed to prevent water dripping to the porch floor below. A collection of watering cans makes a useful as well as a decorative addition to a plant-filled porch.

WARM OR COOL. The color scheme you choose sets the overall mood for the porch. Use light, bright colors such as yellow, orange, or red to brighten the cool light on a dark, north-facing porch. Cool off a sun-drenched porch with darker tones of greens or blues. Or emphasize the natural exposure by using warm tones to make a bright porch even brighter or cooler hues to turn a dark porch into an escape from the sun. As with any color scheme, make a full commitment and carry through with accessories and other details.

Yellows mixed with taupes give this screen porch, *above,* a cheerful, sunny feeling. The simple window treatment consists of striped cotton panels attached to tension rods. The rods

can be adjusted up or down for light control or for privacy. The all-weather wicker chair
features a pullout ottoman. Slip-on back and seat covers dress a folding cafe chair.
A hammock proves an adventurous alternative to a sofa. The hammock should be securely
anchored and stretched tightly for comfort.

■ Shades of green make the porch, *above,* a cool retreat from the summer's heat.
This porch is a canvas and aluminum affair set on an existing wood deck. Commercially
available, such a screened room is an alternative to constructing a porch. Although the
ceiling is canvas, a wood porch ceiling can be painted a dark shade to give a similar effect.

THE RIGHT PIECES. Accessories mean the difference between an ordinary room and a memorable one. That's as true on a porch as it is inside. Choose pieces that reflect you and your family's interests. Finds collected on your travels and family treasures impart extra meaning.

■ Accessories create a big, bold statement on the screened porch, *opposite*. The reds and yellows of the painted canvas floorcloth repeat in the fabrics used for pillows and cushions. The light-leg chairs and glass-top table don't obscure the hand-painted floorcloth. A Moravian star chandelier crafted from tin echoes the center shape of the cloth below. By the door, a whimsical folk art figure greets guests.

■ Art can be anywhere. A pair of carved wood animals, *above left*, accents the stripped pine coffee table. A stone-and-cast-iron table elevates a colorful pitcher and a flower-filled bowl. The sofa folds out to make a bed; the repurposed metal-and-vinyl chair started life as office furniture.

■ A bicycle and a guitar, *above right*, telegraph the owner's varied interests. Adirondack chairs, in a variety of colors, offer a comfortable shape and scale for porch sitting.

■ Floor treatments make a porch seem more like a real room. The pair of small kilim rugs on this porch, *right*, repeats colors and textures of the pillows. Such flat-woven reversible rugs are a good choice as they are easier to clean than pile rugs.

decks

Open, light, and sunny, your deck allows you to enjoy the outside with a minimum of fuss. Keep day-to-day furnishings, such as tables and chairs, simple and durable. Then bring out the accent pieces for special occasions.

Use an eclectic mix of furniture for your deck. Everything doesn't have to match. Instead, look for individual pieces that fit your needs and budget. Spruce up secondhand wood or metal lawn chairs with fresh coats of enamel paint. Add pillows and cushions for comfort and color, small tables for convenience.

For hot summer afternoons, shade is a necessity. An inexpensive natural or colored market umbrella transforms even the most modest deck into a Mediterranean resort. For a more permanent solution, add an arbor over part of the deck. Use plastic screening to gently filter the light.

Decorate your deck or balcony with container plants grouped together for maximum impact. Add a trellis for the shade and color of fast-growing vines. Mount pots and baskets along the railing. Include decorative column caps or finials, available at building supply stores, to give your deck a custom touch.

Grilling outdoors keeps the kitchen cool in summer and allows guests to join in the cooking experience. Install a light above the grill for nighttime use; protect a wood deck with a pad of brick below the grill. Enjoy.

decks & balconies

Use colors and furnishings to welcome friends to your comfortable and inviting outdoor space.

MADE IN THE SHADE. Although a deck by definition has no roof over it, it can be a cool and shady spot, even on the hottest day. Let nature provide the shade. Deciduous trees planted close to the edge can shade the deck through the summer. In winter, they drop their leaves, allowing the sun to warm the deck. When building a deck, work carefully to preserve existing shade trees. Pay particular attention during construction to protect trees and their root systems from damage. If at all possible, do not disturb the ground under existing trees. Don't allow trucks or heavy equipment to park on or near trees; compacting the soil can injure roots.

■ Vines provide a ceiling over this seaside deck, *right*. Posts along one side of the deck support a network of wires stretching to the house. Vines planted in the ground below are trained up the posts and across the wires, creating the canopy of shade. The vine's leaves gently filter the light, creating a delightfully dappled pattern of shadow across the deck. Open on three sides to breezes and directly linked to a screened porch, this deck offers a spot for casual dining day or night. Furnishings are simple and fun. A massive table, built from heavy timbers bolted together, is ample enough to handle six to eight guests. The table, left to weather naturally, has taken on the silver gray of the decking. Galvanized steel chairs prove both comfortable and durable. A matching stool doubles as an end table for an Adirondack chair while three whimsical cutouts are lighthearted additions to the guest list.

ABOVE IT ALL. Located well above the noises of the street, a balcony assures quiet retreat status. With at least a measure of privacy guaranteed by its height, a balcony can be developed as a personal sanctuary for family and close friends. Here is where you can read or nap without fear of interruption. Spend the evening talking quietly in the dark watching the lights of the city below. Here, too, is an idyllic setting for reading the morning newspaper. If a second-floor space is too far from the kitchen for dining, there's no need for a large table. But do provide a cozy spot for a cup of coffee in the morning or dessert with the stars after dinner.

■ This second-floor townhouse balcony, *left,* functions as a family sitting room off the bedrooms. High in the trees, the compact space is furnished as an indoor living area with sofa, chairs, and tables. The outdoor metal furniture features graceful cast ornaments. Glass tabletops keep the look open while allowing a pair of cast-stone birds nesting below the table to be enjoyed from above. An area rug organizes the furniture. Container plants fill every corner; decorative brackets display pots on the corner post.

■ An ornate marble-top table and pair of chairs, *above,* recall Victorian-era ice cream parlors. Set close to the balcony edge, the visually light pieces don't obscure the view through the metal balcony railing. For any deck or balcony, metal offers a thin, less intrusive alternative to a wood railing. Kept painted, it lasts indefinitely.

■ Located off a bedroom, this small balcony, *left,* affords a good place to start the day. The ottoman and chair invite relaxation; a matching side table can hold coffee and magazines. When a balcony connects this readily to an interior room, color and fabric selection need to be coordinated.

COLORS FROM NATURE. For a restful deck that blends with the landscape, choose natural materials and let them weather. (See page 159.) Although the woods used outdoors, such as redwood, cedar, cypress, teak, and treated pine, begin with different appearances, sun and rain change them all to shades of gray. To hurry the process along, special bleaching oil stains can be used on the raw wood. Always test first on a sample to preview the results. Periodic applications of a preservative will prolong the life of unpainted wood, including outdoor furniture. Only wood species, such as redwood, that are naturally resistant to rotting or woods that are treated to prevent decay should be used outdoors without paint protection.

■ A pair of teak benches and matching table, *left,* take on a rich grayish-brown shade when left to weather. An unpainted fence and deck echo the grays and browns of the furniture and of nearby tree branches. An embroidered tablecloth, turned on the diagonal, imparts a touch of elegance. The table and nearby shelf display a collection of rustic miniature buildings.

■ What could be more natural than a deck railing made of logs and limbs? With peeled logs for posts and rails, *above,* the look recalls a mountain cabin. Such railings must meet local building codes, which typically are in the range of 36 or 42 inches. Many codes require pickets be spaced to prevent a 4-inch diameter ball from passing through.

DIFFERENT DECKS, DIFFERENT APPROACHES. Each situation calls for its own individual design solution. Orient your deck for sun, shade, views, or privacy in keeping with your family's needs and the dictates of your site. Remember that not every type of deck is appropriate for every lot. First list your requirements; then think through different ways to meet those needs given the existing site. Check on any zoning restrictions, such as setback lines or fence heights. Analyze the costs of different options and compare them with your budget. Pick the best compromise. If necessary, implement over time.

Decorating a deck is easy when the view is as lovely as this, *below left*. Keep things simple and uncluttered, and place the emphasis on the scenery beyond the deck. Here the unpretentious railing encourages the eye to glide past to the harbor below. To pull the vistas to the water, plants are placed on the outside of the railing.

When the view is lacking, a garden vignette provided by a sideboard, *below right*, creates a focal point. Perched atop the shelf, a pair of cast-stone planters holds miniature cedars. The planters are placed directly over the figures to avoid bending or breaking the glass. Plants cascading over a tall board fence create a living backdrop; a sturdy platform on casters makes moving heavy planters easy. In the corner, supported by a Corinthian column capital, a glass gazing ball lawn ornament reflects the scene.

A large deck such as this one, *above,* divides into separate zones for dining and conversation. Railings and hedges define the areas unified by white paint. A level change also can distinguish one part of the deck from another. This deck incorporates an arbor that supports an Adirondack-style swing, creating a cozy seating area away from the house. Other chairs can be moved about the deck as needed. Lattice panels at the ends of the arbor provide enclosure. Brackets display clay pots on the wall.

OFF TO MARKET. The most flexible and practical way to create shade is with an umbrella. The market umbrella, used for years to shade vendors' stalls in Europe, is an increasingly popular and practical choice. Available in prices from under $100 to over $1,000, the umbrellas feature a sturdy wood frame and a special vent panel at the top that keeps sudden gusts from lifting the umbrella.

■ A striped umbrella shades the table on this formal deck, *above*. Cushions are the same fabric. The chairs, benches, and railings are all in the Chippendale style. This was popularized by the 18th-century English furniture maker Thomas Chippendale, who was influenced by Chinese designs. Americans from the time of Thomas Jefferson have embraced Chippendale motifs.

■ Soft blues for the umbrella, painted country chairs, and serving pieces bring a cool restfulness to the dining deck, *above,* emphasized by the change in deck height. Along one side of the low deck, a railing fitted with cushions provides additional seating. The tailored white tablecloth is trimmed with the same blue-and-white stripe used for the tie-on cushions. A small hole cut in the center of the tablecloth allows the umbrella pole to extend neatly through it and anchor firmly in the base.

■ A market umbrella shades the chaise lounge on this rooftop terrace, *left.* Because market umbrellas cannot be tilted, they need to be positioned close to seating. The teak coffee table from Indonesia holds a pair of oversize glass hurricane lanterns. A mural embellishes the stucco wall with a hand-painted scene. To finish, an ornately detailed rug diagonally tops a larger natural rug.

SHADED IN STYLE. Prized for their shade, umbrellas can be decorative as well as functional. Dress up an umbrella with ribbon or add small lights underneath for a festive accent. (Be sure to remove before closing.) Go bright or subtle with your color choice. Search out an umbrella with a special shape or style to accent your deck. If you have a large deck or a deck and adjacent patio, consider purchasing two umbrellas for zoned seating and dining. Or create your own shade by stretching wires above the deck and adding fabric panels on rings. Slide the fabric on the wires to put shade where you need it. Add an awning to the house to shade part of the deck. A large container tree also can provide shade; equip your container with casters for mobility.

■ Draped in mosquito netting, this white market umbrella, *opposite,* takes on an exotic, romantic feel evocative of an African photography safari. The gossamer cloth simply drapes over the top of the umbrella, then is gathered and tied. When the insects come out, the cloth can be untied and completely wrapped around the umbrella, creating a mosquito-proof tent. The heavy metal base provides a sturdy anchor.

■ A traditional white market umbrella with attractive wood ribs, *left,* diffuses light for this luncheon on the deck. A crisp white tablecloth and white wicker complete the white theme.

■ Recalling the tiny umbrellas used in tropical drinks, this unusual full-size example, *below,* shades the scene. The terrace is gravel, an easy-to-install option when curved or irregular patio shapes are desired. The material works best on a flat site and assures better drainage than a concrete or stone terrace. At least two inches of crushed gravel are required with clay, sand, or crushed oyster shells as a binder.

A gated fence and lush tropical plants enclose the entry deck on this Gulf Coast cottage, *left.* Even though it is at the front of the house, careful siting and the relationship to other houses assure a measure of privacy. In higher-density communities such as this, neighboring houses and garages can be used for screening, often giving more privacy than a neighborhood with large lots and houses spaced far apart. In the foreground, a large urn, fitted with a pump, turns into a gently bubbling fountain. The second-floor balcony offers glimpses of the waves and water.

This tiny deck, *below,* serves as a transition from the doorway to the garden. In addition to protecting the door from the sun, the alcove can be closed off for privacy. The louvered panel is sized to screen a chair set deep in the shade. The canvas curtain can be drawn, allowing the door behind to be opened to the breezes with complete privacy from the street and nearby houses.

DECKS IN SECLUSION. Even though a deck may be open to the sky and sun above, it can be private from the rest of the world. High walls turn a deck into a private courtyard reminiscent of New Orleans. Check local code restrictions. Masonry is the traditional choice for garden walls, but wood fencing often pairs with decks. Although it may take some time to grow, a dense hedge can be every bit as solid as a wall. If you like the idea of natural screening, speed the growing cycle by planting atop an earthen berm or raised bed. Or build a simple wood fence frame, cover with mesh wire, and plant with vines to create a living fence.

Broad steps, *opposite,* lead up to a small deck tucked behind the house. Large enough only for a comfortable chair, the deck still serves as an outdoor retreat. Gray pavers blend with the weathered wood decking. Steps display containers.

GARDEN SPOTS. Plants should be an important part of decorating any deck. Select plants for color, texture, and mass. Before adding any plant, learn how big it will grow and if it needs any special growing conditions or care. If the deck is convenient to the kitchen, consider planting vegetables or herbs in containers. If possible, do not place containers directly on the deck surface where they could stain or discolor the wood. Instead, use terra-cotta spacer blocks, available at most garden centers, to hold pots an inch or two above the deck.

■ Shaded by an arbor and a dark green umbrella, *right,* part of this deck is tailor-made for cool and casual dining. A chaise lounge and a wood and cast-iron garden bench provide spots to enjoy the sun. Everywhere plants soften the hard edges, adding texture and color. A rectangular terra-cotta planter repeats the red of the tablecloth.

■ A model of a wind-powered water pump, *below,* accents the sunny part of the deck. For sunning, a lightweight chaise lounge that folds flat and is easy to move is the best choice. Synthetic rather than natural fabric covers on cushions ensure longest wear.

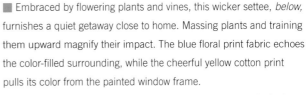

■ Embraced by flowering plants and vines, this wicker settee, *below,* furnishes a quiet getaway close to home. Massing plants and training them upward magnify their impact. The blue floral print fabric echoes the color-filled surrounding, while the cheerful yellow cotton print pulls its color from the painted window frame.

■ Lined up in double rows like spectators at a tennis match, *below left,* a collection of colorful watering cans reiterates the garden style decorating. Other garden-related objects edited from a large collection for special deck display include the trellis leaning against a window and a birdhouse perched on a fern stand. A green-painted board in the back of each chair coordinates with the green-and-white fabric. Sunflowers and flags contribute to the summer fun.

UP ON THE WALL. Bring the walls adjoining a deck to life with found objects used as art. Look for items that lend themselves to mounting on a flat surface, such as tiles, bas-relief plaques, or windows. Objects with more depth can be as interesting but require care in hanging. Anchor heavier items so they are not merely resting on a shelf. Hang with fine wire and inconspicuous hooks.

■ Angels share the walls with a cow skull on this Southwestern deck, *above*. Below the two angels are a mermaid and a hand-shape switchplate. Unusual pillows in a cowboy motif reflect the Western setting, while the weathered coffee table and bleached-out furniture bear witness to the sun-drenched environment. Two custom-made doors contribute their own character.

In an outdoor room with Country French ambience, a fern-filled fireplace translates into a graceful focal point, *above.* An old wood-and-wire birdcage, a flea market find, hangs on the chimney breast. Paired vases form a symmetrical arrangement on either side of an ivy-filled tureen. A section of tree stump, peeled of its bark and painted, forms an unusual occasional table. A metal bistro table, detailed with a scrolled base, serves as a table for the lamp crafted from a glazed olive oil jar. The grouping includes two Country French chairs, softened with plaid cushions, and a corner plant stand.

A wooden basket, *left,* filled with old garden tools and fresh greenery works as a three-dimensional accent when hung on the wall. Such deep pieces should be located so they don't intrude into circulation paths. Because sun can damage items, flea market finds, rather than valuable art, are ideal for deck decorating.

patios

A patio is as much a part of the garden as a part of the house. Combine the amenities of inside with the gracious greenery of outside to make your patio or terrace a garden destination. Anchor a focal point with a piece of garden statuary, an inviting bench, or a fountain to lure visitors to share your creation.

You can't have too many plants. Mass containers of herbs and seasonal color to fill an empty corner. You might even find a spot for a few vegetables. A simple wood bench or larger terra-cotta pots turned upside down give plants extra height. Go even taller with vines trained up a wall.

For privacy, strategically place a tall fence or wall to block a view. Decorate this backdrop with garden art or an espaliered plant. To create an extra sense of enclosure, include a decorative fence with an ornate iron gate or aged shutters. For flexible privacy, pot large shrubs or small trees in wheeled containers. A freestanding outdoor fireplace, fire pit, or chimenea will warm guests on cool nights and extend your enjoyment of the space year-round.

For a festive mood, string miniature white Christmas lights through nearby trees or up a vine-covered wall. Even though it must withstand the weather, your patio can be furnished with comfortable furniture and handy tables. Bring out extra cushions and pillows for dining and relaxing.

patios&terraces

Projecting out into the lush garden, a plant-filled terrace invites guests to dine amid artful finds.

SURROUNDED BY STONE. The warm, natural colors of stone make a terrace seem one with the landscape. On a sloping site, include low retaining walls to create terraced planting beds, define the lawn, or enclose a pool. Walls as high as 3 feet are achievable do-it-yourself projects. Bring in a professional for higher ones. Flagstone walks and terraces can be constructed by laying flat stones on a bed of sand. Fit the pieces together, leaving narrow joints between. Carefully level each stone and fill in with sand-mix mortar. For an even more permanent surface, first pour a concrete slab, then set the stones in mortar on top of the slab. Stone, tile, and brick also offer good ways to resurface an existing concrete terrace or walk. With any type of masonry surface, slope about ¼ inch per foot for drainage; walks should be crowned slightly for drainage. Because shipping is expensive, use local stone as a budget-stretcher if at all possible.

An old set of lawn furniture, repainted to blend with the stone, turns this flagstone terrace into a delightful outdoor dining space, *right*. The spring steel back and seat are surprisingly comfortable, even without cushions. Properly primed and painted, steel or iron outdoor furniture can remain outside indefinitely. Each piece should be checked carefully every few months for signs of rust; rusted areas should be sanded down, primed, and painted with outdoor enamel. A coat of paste wax offers additional protection from the elements. For parties and other special occasions, a colorful tablecloth in a Country French print and rustic candleholders illustrate the casually elegant touches appropriate to alfresco dining. Collections, such as Greek temple architectural models, and weather-aged pots and garden elements, impart their own charms to an understated setting reminiscent of France or Italy.

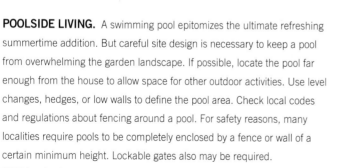

POOLSIDE LIVING. A swimming pool epitomizes the ultimate refreshing summertime addition. But careful site design is necessary to keep a pool from overwhelming the garden landscape. If possible, locate the pool far enough from the house to allow space for other outdoor activities. Use level changes, hedges, or low walls to define the pool area. Check local codes and regulations about fencing around a pool. For safety reasons, many localities require pools to be completely enclosed by a fence or wall of a certain minimum height. Lockable gates also may be required.

■ This raised porch provides a shady spot overlooking the sunny pool, *above.* Broad steps lead down to the open stone terrace that wraps the pool. A pool house is conveniently located on the lower terrace. The cast-concrete pool edging blends with the colors of the stone terrace.

■ An awning such as this one, *left,* represents an easy and surprisingly affordable way to add shade. Local companies often provide a range of colors, sizes, shapes, and brackets. Retractable or roll-out awnings allow the option of shade or sun. If possible, the awning color should repeat the color of the house's trim or roof. The front panel can be plain or decorative. Here the scallop pattern echoes the shape of the roof tiles.

■ Plant-filled pots, *opposite below,* line the edge of the covered terrace. Their deep blue glaze contrasts with the warm reddish browns of the trim. A bas-relief cast-stone plaque adds a durable accent to the wall.

■ Shaded by the porch, the raised terrace, *below,* affords a place out of the sun yet close to the pool. The wheeled chaise lounge rolls out easily. Louvered shutters allow the interior rooms to be closed for privacy.

DINING OUT. Moving the table into the garden illustrates a way to spice up even the most ordinary meal. The food can be as simple or as elaborate as you want. Served outside with fresh air, sunshine, and a gentle breeze, the meal will be memorable. For practicality, locate any outdoor dining area as close as possible to the kitchen. A table too far away will seldom be used. Try to avoid level changes; negotiating steps while loaded with dishes can be difficult or even dangerous. A second, smaller table nearby can be used as a buffet or bar or to stack dishes after the meal. Include dry storage nearby for tablecloths, cushions, pillows, and other outdoor accessories.

■ Crisp white linens contrast with black-painted furniture on a small stone terrace, *above*. Roses, silver, and china turn morning coffee into a special occasion. An outdoor table should be checked carefully to make sure it is free of rust, dirt, or rough areas before topping with linens.

■ Ready for a party, this terrace, *above,* is large enough to accommodate three round tables for luncheons or dinner parties and a smaller table for books and accessories. Normally, only one dining table is in place; the other table and chairs are folded and stored away. Before setting the table for meals or serving, make sure it is level to avoid tipping over. Often merely rotating an outdoor table is enough to eliminate a wobble. If not, a leg or legs can be shimmed (leveled) with a short piece of wood shingle or the old restaurant standby, a book of matches.

■ Windows cut into the stuccoed masonry wall, *left,* frame views while assuring a measure of privacy inside. Tall trellises emphasize the height of the wall. The rectangular table seats six comfortably, but its glass top and light steel frame provide an open look that makes it seem smaller than it actually is. For outdoor serving, an easy-to-carry tray is a welcome addition.

Simple, almost austere, this high-ceiling garden room, *opposite,* illustrates the Zen serenity of clean, contemporary design. A square window, set high on the wall, brings in light from above to emphasize the high ceiling. Large squares of stone form the floor and flow outside to become a garden walk. Four wicker chairs and a pair of matching ottomans are the only seating. Ornate cast planters, painted to match the pale walls, flank the door.

Hidden behind a pair of louvered garden gates, the cobblestone terrace leads to a private guesthouse, *below.* The stones, laid in continuous slightly wavy rows, exaggerate the distance from the gate to the getaway. Garden statuary, a pair of urns, and topiary trees enhance the vista.

BACKYARD RETREATS. A garden getaway, located away from the main house, represents a special escape. It can be a pool house, a guesthouse, or a pavilion. Use it for entertaining, for weekend guests, or as a place to vacation without ever leaving home. Keep the basic floor plan simple and open for maximum flexibility—uses change over time. A guest house might be needed for an elderly parent or a child home from college or even as a home office. Check with local regulations before adding a bath or kitchen, though, as some municipalities don't allow separate apartments in residential areas.

Open and bright, this outdoor pavilion, *above,* is comfortable for friends or cozy for two. The soft, pale colors of its natural wood construction ensure a soothing backdrop. Weathered teak chairs and a clean-lined coffee table blend with the neutrals. Wicker with matching cushions adds a chic touch.

SERENE NEUTRALS. Create an escape with a soft palette that's as restful outside as in. Work with shades ranging from white and pale cream to deep tan and taupe.

▓ Colors from off-white to pale yellow soothe the fresh-air room, *above,* with a calm, sophisticated air. Skylights set between massive beams open the indoor-outdoor room to the sun. For the coffee table, weathered timbers support a limestone slab. A collection of glass hurricanes introduces shape and height without color. Darker accents, such as the wood box, candleholders, fan, and mirror frames, are brown, not black, to reduce the contrast against the pale walls.

▓ The exposed beams visually form an arbor over this poolside terrace, *right.* Doors open inward to protect them from the weather and to avoid blocking the terrace outside. The market umbrella poolside serves as a destination, drawing the eye and the visitor into the landscape.

■ Wide French doors, flanked by sidelights, open the bedroom to an adjoining terrace, *above.* Roll-down matchstick blinds above the glass ensure privacy when needed. Set at the same level as the bedroom floor, the terrace is accessible and inviting. Careful coordination of colors in both spaces produces a harmonious blend. The rolled arms of the all-weather wicker chosen for the outdoors echo the scale of the armchair inside. The generously sized bedside table holds plenty of books for indoor or outdoor reading.

■ The light tans of natural wood, *left,* preserve the natural theme. The folding chairs can store away when not in use. A rectangular table similar to this can rest atop sawhorse-like supports, yet come apart for storage. Even the wood serving bowl, cheese tray, and softly glazed olive oil jar contribute to the subtle scheme. The loose arrangement of native foliage reflects the location in Northern California.

DESERT DELIGHTS. A walled courtyard, called a patio, is a traditional feature of Spanish architecture that influenced styles of the desert Southwest. It offers shelter from the wind and sun and from the noise of the street. In this protected place, plants grow, and flowers blossom, creating an oasis in the desert. With such assets, a walled courtyard is an undeniable pleasure. If the concept works for your location, choose wall material to coordinate with your house and others in the neighborhood. Soften the hard lines of a wall with climbing vines.

■ A tile-and-terra-cotta fountain, *right,* visually anchors the patio. The sound of water is refreshing, especially in an arid climate. Although the exterior of the fountain is clad in warm red tile to match the colors of the patio, cool cobalt blue tiles line the pool. A round table with a deep purple fringe skirt pairs with ornate bleached chairs that recall the Spanish Colonial influence.

■ Desert flowers and plants, massed along a stone retaining wall, *opposite above,* splash a sea of color. The weathered table and chairs stay outside year-round. Cushions and colorful cloths are easily added.

■ Notched in the adobe wall, this outdoor room, *opposite below,* provides shade and comfort on the edge of the patio. For continuity, the same basket-weave brick pavers repeat for both spaces. Brick is grouted for the enclosed area, but on the patio it's set in sand to allow rainwater to drain. Seating consists of a simple L-shape bench.

ABOVE IT ALL. Rooftop terraces afford views, plenty of sun, and an escape from the street. In an urban setting where lots are small and houses close together, going up may be the only option for outdoor privacy. At the coast or lake, a terrace or tower may offer the best views of the sunset over the water. Before adding any type of rooftop structure, check with local building officials about height restrictions or other limits. Check to see that the structure below can carry the extra load. Do provide some shade; it can get hot and glary up on the roof.

■ This tower retreat on the coast, *above,* guarantees views of the water and the surrounding rooftops. In this development, small rooftop terraces and towers are encouraged. A settee, rather than a sofa, reflects the scale. Matching cushions unify the wicker pieces. A flat-weave rug in subtle browns blends with the flooring.

■ On this rooftop, *above,* stuccoed walls form a solid and very private railing. A high table and tall stools create an outdoor bar to enjoy coffee at sunrise or drinks at sunset. The high, solid walls convey a sense of safety and enclosure, important in a location well above the ground. Because it is a flat, uniform surface, the painted golden-yellow wall serves as a neutral backdrop for plants and garden statuary. Durable kilim rugs introduce color and exotic pattern to the floor as well as to the skirt for the bistro table.

■ Welded from steel tubing, the railing, *left,* is open and light to avoid blocking the view. The concentric square panels alternate with decorative cast-iron panels. Topiary trees, trimmed poodle-fashion and planted in European containers, frame a wicker planter filled with gardenias and garden statuary in this formal arrangement. The floral rug echoes the old-fashioned appeal of the antique wicker.

bark, not nuggets, and use only on relatively flat sites. Here a section of salvaged picket fence becomes a backdrop for the bench. To duplicate the look with a new fence, brush on thinned paint and wipe with a rag. Repeat with slightly different colors for the desired effect.

■ Plants fill this rooftop terrace, *below,* and climb skyward on simple wood trellises and arbors. In any garden, and especially on a rooftop one, think three-dimensionally. Here simple trellises become flower-filled walls. Vines strung on wires frame the small porch, and flower boxes accent the windows. Two small tables fit better into the space than a single large one. The small tables also offer more flexibility, allowing dining for two, four, or eight guests.

■ The sound of water is a pleasant addition to any garden. A simple fountain made from an old hand pump and a galvanized bucket animates this small terrace, *opposite.* The base is a stepped box made from plywood paneling. An inexpensive electric pump in the bucket recirculates the water. Submersible pumps can be found in the garden section of most home center stores.

FOR THE GARDENER. Working in the garden should be a relaxing pastime. What better way to reward a morning's chores than a quiet place to sit and survey your efforts. A solitary chair or bench set just off a path provides a spot to stop and enjoy the smells and sounds. If possible, locate several seating areas around the garden so one will always be in shade. Include seating near, or even within, a vegetable garden. It's the perfect place to enjoy a fresh-from-the-vine watermelon. Create a shady tepee from bamboo poles and climbing beans.

■ A simple seat and crude bench, framed by container trees, *above,* furnish a pleasant resting spot for the busy gardener. The path is pine bark mulch, an inexpensive material that blends naturally with the landscape. To avoid washing, buy shredded

entertaining

Any meal served outside can be special. Fresh flowers clipped minutes before dining, the smells of food grilling, the sound of birds chirping, and the taste of homegrown tomatoes can't be duplicated in a restaurant. **At home, it's easy.**

Accent your table with a centerpiece from your garden. Fill a galvanized watering can with a simple, yet colorful bouquet. Use containers of live flowers, interwoven with greenery, to decorate a long table or buffet. For a **relaxed, casual get-together,** repurpose galvanized tubs to ice down beverages, new terra-cotta pots to hold napkins and utensils, and Mason jars for iced tea. **On a more elegant, formal occasion,** bring out your finest china, crystal, and silver serving pieces. **The choice is yours.** To accommodate a large group, folding card tables, **disguised with floor-length tablecloths,** can spill across the lawn. For a European touch, set a wood farm table and arrange chairs brought from inside the house.

Subtle lighting helps set the mood and avoid insects. If you don't have dimmers, swap the existing lightbulbs for lower-wattage ones. **The flicker of candles always makes dining more elegant.** Ring the porch with votives, cluster cylinders or tapers on the table, or hang an inexpensive candle chandelier. **To keep the flame from going out** and for safety, protect a candle used outdoors with a glass chimney or other decorative container.

entertainingout

Invite your guests into the garden or bring your garden to your guests with plant-filled spaces.

ACCENT WITH PLANTS. If the intent is to create a space that evokes the spirit of the garden, then you can't have too many plants. But choose them carefully, as you would any other accessory. Consider the color—not all greens are the same. The texture of a plant is also important; plants with large leaves can visually dominate a room. The shape, height, and fullness also must be kept in mind. Learn the growth habits of a plant. Does it grow up or out or cascade down? Does it need to be staked? Will it grow too big for the space? And most important, select plants that can thrive in the location. Light levels, humidity, and temperature must all be considered. Once the plants are in place, develop a habit of routine maintenance to keep your plants healthy and flourishing. As an alternative to living plants, consider plant art. Posters or prints from a botanical garden or art museum often are inexpensive. Paintings by local artists can be affordable; some artists will undertake a commissioned painting. Botanical prints or pages clipped from a calendar can be matted and framed. Group identically framed prints together for maximum impact.

■ Plants, both real and painted, fill this formal screened porch, *right.* The soft beige fabrics used for the tablecloth, upholstered armchairs, and window treatments provide a neutral canvas for the greenery. A giant hand-painted pear graces the table skirt; the decorative fringe is a green chosen to match the colors of the pear. The glass top protects the skirt's fabric from the inevitable spill. Mahogany chairs serve as frames for two more botanical paintings on the silk seat backs. All three designs are based on the work of Basilius Besler, a 17th-century botanist and illustrator. In the corners, ficus trees add height.

UNITED BY DESIGN. When a space is large, especially if it is used for both sitting and dining, the entire porch needs to pull together. Wall, floor, and ceiling colors should carry through for unity. Choose furniture that works together. Pieces don't have to match exactly, but they shouldn't differ jarringly. The fabric selected for pillows and cushions unifies the space as well, but there's no need to use one fabric exclusively in a room.

■ In the sitting area, *left,* blue-green rattan pieces are clustered around a custom-painted floorcloth. A similar floorcloth defines the dining area at the other end of the screened porch. Instead of the usual canvas, the work is done on the back side of linoleum, which lies flat, takes paint well, and is durable underfoot. A hand-painted border repeats the geometric pattern on the floorcloth. A stylized painting hangs above the sofa.

■ The faux bamboo dining chairs, *above,* painted to match the rattan, recall Chippendale designs. Tiny topiaries share a baker's rack with the wine. Hand-painted shades on the chandelier repeat the topiary theme. The same yellow-with-white-trim colors of the exterior repeat for the porch.

ELEGANCE ON THE PORCH. As these examples attest, a screen porch transforms into a gracious place for entertaining that can be fun as well as formal. Combine more formal elements, such as skirted tables and upholstered chairs, with elements from the garden. ■ A pair of slipper chairs, hand-painted with garden scenes, gathers around a glass-topped pedestal table, *right*. A large cast-stone urn or column, available at garden centers, could work for a similar table base. For stability, the base should be at least one-third the diameter of the top. A 36-inch-diameter table is a good size for two to four guests.

■ The iron chandelier, *opposite below,* interjects a light, yet elegant touch. One way to choose the size of a chandelier is to measure the length and width of the room in feet and add together. The chandelier would be that number of inches in width. (For example, a 12×20-foot room would need a 32-inch-diameter fixture.) The bottom of the chandelier should be 30 inches above the top of the table if the ceiling height is 8 feet, and placed an inch higher for each additional foot of ceiling height.

■ Ivy-covered trellises repeat the curved shape and emphasize the high ceiling, *above.* A graceful wrought-iron bench, set on the diagonal, fills a corner. A column capital from Syria serves as the coffee table. The dining chairs take their design inspiration from a Greek Revival railing pattern. A tall bronze vase elevates a rose-filled bouquet above the skirted table.

■ Flowers surround the table, *left,* evoking a garden feel. The table is set with an unusual china pattern featuring a chair motif. In a delightfully ironic twist, the pillows depict china teapots and vases.

KEEP THE CENTER SIMPLE. For a light, easy, yet dramatic centerpiece, think simple. Nothing tops a generous arrangement of fresh-cut flowers from the garden. Use a simple, plain container to showcase the flowers, not the container. Glass cylinders, white ceramic vases and pitchers, silver bowls, urns, and natural straw baskets work well with almost any type of flower or color scheme.

■ A simple glass cylinder, filled with fresh-cut hydrangea, makes a chic centerpiece for this porch table, *opposite*. On the inside, a pair of of taller glass cylinders brimming with green apples flanks a copper pot overflowing with greenery. When the whole house is opened for a party, coordinate decoration inside and out. Oversize white napkins double as place mats for the glass-topped table. Glass is a popular tabletop choice for porches because it is impervious to moisture, easy to clean, and imparts a light, open look that blends with any style.

■ Even the tiniest table benefits from an arrangement of fresh flowers. Here a basket holds a mix of flowering and green plants; another basket contains caladiums, *below*. Houseplants with decorative leaves, such as caladiums, are a long-lasting alternative to cut flowers. Pillows and a cushion add a touch of color and comfort to the painted porch rocker. Polka-dot ties accent one pillow.

ADD A SWEEP OF FABRIC. Fabric offers an easy way to introduce color and pattern to a porch. Use it to soften a hard edge, screen a view, or add a hint of mystery and romance to an ordinary space. Choose a simple stripe or solid in subtle shades or bolder hues, or opt for patterns that reflect your personality. For long life, buy fabric that withstands the weather and cleans easily.

■ Simple tiebacks frame the openings on this dining and sitting porch, *above*. The striped fabric is mounted to rods set between the porch columns. Rings allow the draperies to be pulled closed for privacy or opened for light and air. A latticework screen at the end ensures additional privacy for nighttime dining. Four wicker captain's chairs create a flexible and easy-to-rearrange grouping for conversation. The tall folding tray serves as a coffee table. Buttons detail the solid white pillows in a tailored style.

■ A table skirt elegantly refines the most ordinary table. Framed by a pair of folding steel chairs, this skirted table, *opposite,* proves the right size for breakfast for two. The braid-and-tasseled trim embellishes the plain cloth. Ready-made skirts are available in a range of sizes and fabrics. If a table skirt is custom-made, the finished diameter should be equal to the diameter of the table plus twice its height. The hem requires extra fabric; cording or piping may be added.

■ Gossamer fabric substitutes for insect screening on this front porch, *above.* Although the porch is not completely enclosed, the fabric blocks much of the open area. Rods at the top support the panels; an arrangement of cords and pulleys allows the panels to be pulled back. The cord ties are placed high, leaving the lower portion free to blow in the breeze. The skirt on the serving piece features a box pleat. The same fabric is used to edge the floorcloth.

DINING ALONG THE PORCH. When the space is large, break it into intimate areas for dining or conversation. For smaller gatherings, guests can move from the table to more comfortable seating for after-dinner conversation. Fort a larger party, set up the dining table for buffet-style serving and let guests gather in small groups on the porch, in the garden, or inside. Arrange plenty of coffee tables and end tables so guests don't have to balance their plates on their knees.

■ Colors of furniture and fabric unify this long screened porch while subtle lighting softly illuminates the scene, *opposite*. With generous space, guests have a number of seating options. For flexibility, lightweight chairs can be pulled into position as needed. Wall-mounted sconces, crafted in old-fashion lantern style, are an excellent lighting choice for the porch. Table lamps and candles balance the illumination.

■ Topped with a white cloth, this wicker hamper, *above,* converts into a coffee table. Taller serving pieces, at least 18 inches high, allow guests to serve themselves with a minimum of bending. White napkins and tablecloths, available at restaurant supply stores, are an always-appropriate alternative to colored or patterned linens. White plates, clear glass serving pieces, and silver accents finish a gracious setting in style.

SKIRTING THE ISSUE. Select a table skirt to introduce color and pattern to a garden room without the expense of adding a new piece of furniture. Paired with a piece of plywood, a skirt can enlarge or even change the shape of an existing table. Best of all, a full-length skirt hides less-than-attractive or damaged tables.

■ Tie-on cushions ensure comfort for these cane-bottom side chairs, *right.* The stylized leaf pattern creates a strong graphic effect. Black rope ties with black and white tassels wrap the rear legs. The table skirt itself is a black and white toile.

■ A soft yellow-green overcloth, *below,* provides a solid backdrop for patterned china and napkins. Using an overcloth, also called a napkin or table square, allows an easy change of color.

A muted plaid square skirt softens a metal outdoor table, *above*. Soft pastel colors blend more easily in the garden than bright, intense hues. Between parties, a skirt can remain safely folded away in a drawer while the table suffers the effects of rain and sun. Here coordinated floral fabric covers the generously sized pillows in the chairs. Contrasting smaller pillows could be added for accents. Vines casually twine a tiered plate stand used as a server.

Even the simplest items heighten the sense of joy and beauty in a garden setting. A white pottery pitcher, *left*, filled with flowers from the garden, rests atop a rusted steel and glass shelf. Tag sales and flea markets are sources for such shapely but inexpensive finds to hold summer flowers from the garden or flower shop.

ONTO THE LAWN. When you don't have a deck or terrace, take the table out onto the lawn. For a wedding or other special occasion, the lawn offers an excellent way to handle an overflow of tables. Rent extra tables and chairs, or pull ones from inside for temporary use. Prop a sheet of plywood on two sawhorses and drape a full-length skirt to create an instant table or server. Folding chairs from an office supply store can be painted to cover basic beige.

■ What could be simpler than the outdoor party scene, *above*. The table is an old door, with peeling paint and hinges still in place. The metal base, now rusted, once held a glass top. The kitchen chairs are lightweight, comfortable, and easy to find at antique or secondhand furniture stores. If a matching set can't be found, mix and match. The two wood urns used for table decorations were salvaged from an old house.

■ With tree limbs for legs, this table, *opposite*, interjects a rustic twist to a garden pavilion. Made of rough boards and edged with twigs, the top holds a spread of fruit, bread, cheese, and wine. Fabric printed with drawings of old garden benches frames the structure. Above the table hangs a reproduction of a late 18th-century candle hall light.

BY SOFT LIGHT. The flickering glow of candles enhances the mood of a romantic occasion. For maximum effect, mass candles on a table or select fixtures that hold several candles above the table. One advantage of candles or lanterns is portability. With nothing to plug in, you can bring light easily to the farthest corner of the garden. Always use a glass votive cup, hurricane shade, or other cover to keep the wind from blowing out a candle. Because rain will dampen the wick, store candles under cover or bring them inside when not in use.

▓ Fanciful fruit ornaments, *opposite,* hang from an iron chandelier. Candle-power chandeliers and other candle-power fixtures usually are less expensive than electrified ones, but they can be harder to find. Garden shops and antique stores are

sources for both new and old fixtures. The same rules apply for hanging height as with interior fixtures (see page 127).

▓ This bamboo tiki torch, *above,* illustrates easy-to-move light for outdoor parties. Staked torches can light a garden path, or when placed around the edge of a terrace, illuminate for dining and dancing.

▓ An ivy-wrapped wire stand holds candles high above the table, *left.* The base of the stand firmly anchors in the ivy-filled clay pot. Using candlesticks or stands to hold the lights above seated eye level assures cross-table conversations are easier and less glary.

decoratingideas

porch&deckprojects

Decorate your fresh-air space as a true living room for relaxing and dining whether you use your porch or deck much of the year or only seasonally. Think of easy projects such as wall-hung art and lamps that impart personality and indoor comforts. Lamps are an easy addition that create soft lighting at night in contrast to brighter overhead porch lights. Other easy add-ons include decorative screens and draperies for privacy and definition, and festive painted floorcloths or tablecloths. When you have more time, dress up your porch with a painted floor in a diamond or other classic motifs, or use the whimsical design of your choice. If you'd like to try your woodworking skill, craft a daybed porch swing for the ultimate relaxing retreat.

VINTAGE FLOOR LAMP BASE

SKILL LEVEL

Beginner

TIME

1 to 2 hours

SUPPLIES

- Vintage or reproduction floor lamp base
- Tulip-shaped shade
- Hot-glue gun
- Glue sticks
- Crafts glue
- Spray fixative
- Fringe

VINTAGE FLOOR LAMP BASE

■ **Choose a tulip shape to refresh a basic lamp base.** Hot glue fringe to the shade. Or if you prefer, cover the shade with fabric or wallpaper. Glue to the shade with crafts glue. Allow to dry, then seal with a spray fixative.

PLANT STANDS
SKILL LEVEL
Beginner
TIME
1 to 2 hours
SUPPLIES
- Small chairs and tables
- Birdcages
- Stands
- Sandpaper
- Tack cloths
- Enamel paint
- Paintbrushes

PLANT STANDS
- **Look for interesting items to convert to plant stands.** Use small chairs to elevate potted plants. Or try birdcages, stands, or small tables for other interesting displays. If necessary, brush off loose paint, sand, and wipe with tack cloths.
- **Refresh with enamel paint** in your color choice, if desired.

TABLE COLLECTIONS

SKILL LEVEL

Beginner

TIME

1 hour per table (not counting collecting)

SUPPLIES FOR PADDED BENCH TABLE

- Padded bench
- Fine sandpaper
- Tack cloths
- Latex paint
- 1-inch paintbrush
- Dresser scarf
- Dresser mirror
- Small collectibles (flower frogs shown here)

SUPPLIES FOR GLASS-TOP TABLE

- Glass-top table or small table with ½-inch glass cut to fit
- Postcard or seed packet collection
- Latex paint (if repainting)

TABLE COLLECTIONS

■ **To make a deeper table for display,** remove the top of a padded bench. Sand the wood, wipe with tack cloths, and repaint in your color choice. Allow to dry and sand lightly for an aged and distressed look. Add a decorative dresser scarf for fabric softness and top with a dresser mirror. Use to display collectibles such as the flower frogs shown here.

■ **If the table is stained,** sand, wipe with tack cloths, and repaint in white or another fresh outdoor color. For postcards or seed packets, arrange on tabletop under glass.

■ **Don't glue the items down** so you can change out your collection.

OCEAN LOVER'S RETREAT PORCH FOLDING SCREEN

SKILL LEVEL

Intermediate

TIME

2 to 3 days to allow for drying

SUPPLIES

- Three, 32×80-inch hollow-core interior doors
- White latex paint
- Four hinges
- Three shades of interior latex paint
- 2-inch wide paintbrush
- 1-inch paintbrush
- Pencil (optional)

OCEAN LOVER'S RETREAT PORCH FOLDING SCREEN

- **Base-coat the doors white.**
- **Hinge doors together.** Paint simple wave shapes with one of your three color choices. Fill in with the remaining colors, adding white to lighten and create subtle color changes with each brushstroke.
- **Allow to dry.** Highlight the wave shapes with the white paint.

OCEAN LOVER'S RETREAT PORCH DRAPERIES

- **Staple fabric to the wood trim,** folding over the top to hide the cut edge. To make tasseled tiebacks, bunch the raffia to about 1 inch in diameter.
- **Tie the center of the bundle** with four pieces of raffia. Lift the bundle by the raffia ties (folding the bundle in half). Bind the top with another piece of raffia.
- **Trim the tassel ends** with sharp scissors.
- **Knot raffia ties** together around the drapery.

OCEAN LOVER'S RETREAT PORCH TABLE

- **Attach grass skirts to the edge** of the tabletop with the staple gun. Place the 36-inch-square overlay on top.

OCEAN LOVER'S RETREAT PORCH DRAPERIES

SKILL LEVEL

Beginner

TIME

1 hour

SUPPLIES

- Staple gun
- 6 yards of 54-inch-wide fabric (lightweight or sheer cotton or linen blend)
- Raffia
- Scissors

OCEAN LOVER'S RETREAT PORCH TABLE

SKILL LEVEL

Beginner

TIME

15 minutes

SUPPLIES

- Four grass skirts (from party or costume shop)
- Ready-to-assemble particleboard table
- Staple gun
- Hawaiian print fabric (36 inches square)

URBAN ROOFTOP DECK PLANTERS WITH TRELLIS

SKILL LEVEL

Beginner

TIME

2 hours

SUPPLIES

- Two shades of yellow latex paint
- 16-ounce plastic measuring cup
- Two plastic mixing buckets
- Two wooden tub planters
- Disposable paintbrushes
- Potting soil
- Six, 6-foot bamboo sticks
- Summer vines
- Rope
- Four, 3- to 4-foot bamboo sticks
- Raffia
- Hot-glue gun
- Glue sticks

URBAN ROOFTOP DECK PLANTERS WITH TRELLIS

- **Dilute paint with water** in proportion of ⅓ paint to ⅔ water. Paint individual boards on the tub with alternating colors. Allow to dry.
- **Fill with potting soil.** Evenly space three, 6-foot bamboo sticks in each tub. Secure at the top with rope. Create horizontal elements by cutting smaller bamboo sticks and attaching with raffia and hot glue.
- **Plant with fast-growing** summer vines.

URBAN ROOFTOP DECK PAINTED TABLECLOTH

SKILL LEVEL
Beginner
TIME
3 to 4 hours
SUPPLIES
- Ready-made round tablecloth
- Tailor's chalk
- Three or four shades of latex paint

URBAN ROOFTOP DECK PAINTED FLOOR

SKILL LEVEL
Intermediate
TIME
2 days, based on drying time
SUPPLIES
- Three shades of exterior oil deck paint
- Straightedge
- Pencil
- Mineral spirits
- 1½-inch blue painter's tape

URBAN ROOFTOP DECK PAINTED TABLECLOTH

- **Draw concentric circles** on tablecloth with tailor's chalk. Paint random bands of colors within each circle, leaving some of the tablecloth fabric unpainted. Use three or four colors and mix together to create a random range of colors.

URBAN ROOFTOP DECK PAINTED FLOOR

- **Paint the entire deck** with darkest shade. Allow to dry thoroughly. Using a pencil and a straightedge, draw a diagonal grid over the entire deck and tape off. Note: the square in the intersection will be taped off and painted separately.
- **Use the two remaining colors** to paint each square, alternating colors to create a checkerboard effect. Let dry. Remove tape.
- **Tape off the intersection** of the bands to make a small square, and paint with a mixture of the two lighter colors. Let dry. Remove tape.
- **Mix 1 cup of the base color** with ¼-cup mineral spirits to create a glaze. Brush over the entire deck to tone down colors and add brushstroke texture.

NATURAL ELEMENTS DRAPERY PANELS

SKILL LEVEL

Intermediate

TIME

2 hours

SUPPLIES

- Bamboo poles (purchased from nursery or garden supply and cut to fit opening)
- Closet rod holder hardware and bracket
- Lightweight fabric
- Scissors
- Iron and ironing board
- Sewing machine
- Thread
- Twine or ribbon for tiebacks

NATURAL ELEMENTS DRAPERY PANELS

- **Install bamboo pole** with a closet rod holder. Hang a bracket support to prevent sagging.
- **Measure width of opening** and divide by two. Multiply by 1½, 2, or 2½, depending upon the amount of fullness desired, and add 1 inch for doubled ¼-inch hems. Measure length from pole to floor. Add 4 inches. Cut two fabric panels with these measurements. Press under ¼ inch twice at the sides and bottom and stitch. Press top under ½ inch, then 3 inches. Stitch close to lower fold to create rod pocket.
- **Sew matching tiebacks** from scraps. Or if you prefer, purchase similar drapery panels in a style compatible with your porch.
- **As an alternative** for a rustic-style porch, substitute twine for fabric tiebacks. Ribbon also works for a dressier look.

NATURAL ELEMENTS FLOORCLOTH

SKILL LEVEL

Intermediate

TIME

3 to 4 days, depending on drying times

SUPPLIES

- Primer
- Vinyl remnant
- Paint roller
- Off-white and tan exterior latex paint
- Pencil
- Straightedge
- 1½-inch blue masking tape
- Crafts knife
- 2-inch flat brush
- Satin-finish polyurethane
- Squeegee

NATURAL ELEMENTS FLOORCLOTH

- **Prime the back of a vinyl remnant** from a home center. Allow to dry. Roll on off-white latex paint. Allow to dry. Using a pencil and straightedge, draw a grid of 1-foot squares. Tape off every other square in the first row. Skip a row; repeat taping odd-numbered rows.
- **For a comb,** cut ¼-inch notches from a squeegee. Brush tan paint in the first square. Pull comb through the square. Wipe paint from the comb. Work in smooth, even motions with a firm stroke. Practice first on scrap to perfect the look you want when dry. Tape off uncombed squares and repeat the same technique for even-numbered rows to form a checkerboard pattern.
- **Apply paint** to uncombed squares of checkerboard. Pull comb at a right angle to previous combing direction. Drag comb through paint again, across the lines just combed. Wipe the comb after every drag to avoid paint accumulating in the notches.
- **Immediately place the comb in the original position** and pull through paint in a zigzag motion. This makes a herringbone pattern. Repeat the technique for unpainted squares without disturbing still-wet squares. Allow to dry. Remove the tape. Seal with two coats of satin-finish polyurethane.

PATTERNED PORCH DIAMOND FLOOR

SKILL LEVEL

Intermediate

TIME

6 to 8 days, depending on drying time

SUPPLIES

- Garden hose
- Scrub brush
- Concrete cleaner and etcher
- Eye protection
- Heavy-duty latex gloves
- Two colors of concrete stain (water-reducible acrylic)
- Paint roller
- Tray
- Yardstick
- Pencil
- Straightedge
- Blue painter's tape

PATTERNED PORCH DIAMOND FLOOR

- **Clean the concrete porch floor with water.** Scrub if necessary to remove grime. Allow to dry. Apply concrete cleaner and etcher per directions on container.
- **Choose two colors of concrete stain.** Roll on the lighter color. Allow to dry. Repeat this base coat.
- **Determine the size of the diamonds** and how they will be placed on the floor. Measure with a yardstick, and mark width and length points. Draw diamonds with a straightedge and pencil by matching the marked points.
- **Tape to the outside or inside of alternating diamonds.** Paint the darker color in checkerboard fashion. Repeat if color is uneven.
- **Allow to dry for 72 hours;** pull off tape.
- **Wait 30 days for paint to set** before placing heavy furniture or pots on the porch.

PATTERNED PORCH POLKA DOT CUSHION FABRIC

SKILL LEVEL
Intermediate

TIME
3 to 4 days, depending on drying time

SUPPLIES
- Pre-washed white cotton fabric
- Scissors
- Newspaper and brown kraft paper (to absorb paint)
- Acrylic yellow paint
- Assorted colors of acrylic paint
- Textile medium
- Disposable foam plate
- Artist's brushes, including ¾-inch brush
- Circle template
- Pencil
- Gold fabric pen

PATTERNED PORCH POLKA DOT CUSHION FABRIC

- **Cut the prewashed fabric** into the cushion shape, including seam allowance. Cover worktable with newspaper, topped by several layers of brown kraft paper. Mix acrylic yellow paint with textile medium, following directions on the medium bottle. Stir well. Brush paint on the fabric so it seeps through to the underside. Allow fabric to dry thoroughly.
- **With a circle template,** draw random polka dots over the fabric. Cover the fabric in an overall pattern for the most interesting look. Mix your polka-dot accent colors with acrylic medium. Stir before painting, as mixed paint tends to separate.
- **With a ¾-inch brush,** fill in outlined polka dots with the paint mixtures. Allow to dry. Outline each polka dot with a gold fabric pen.
- **Air-dry for 24 hours.** Heat-set according to directions on the medium bottle.
- **Sew pillows** as desired.

STRIPED FLOOR
SKILL LEVEL
Beginner
TIME
2 days due to drying time
SUPPLIES
- Trisodium phosphate (TSP) or general-purpose detergent
- Bucket
- Scrub brush
- Garden hose
- Two shades of opaque stain
- 2-inch flat paintbrushes

STENCILED TABLECLOTH
SKILL LEVEL
Beginner
TIME
2 to 3 hours
SUPPLIES
- Solid-color tablecloth
- Stencil plastic
- Stencil tape
- Tracing paper
- Fine-tip marker
- Crafts knife
- Cutting mat
- Stencil paint
- Stencil brush

EASY DRESS-UP STRIPED FLOOR
- **Scrub your deck** with trisodium phosphate **(TSP)** or a general-purpose detergent. Allow to dry thoroughly.
- **Choose two shades** of opaque stain compatible with your siding or brick color. Alternate stains for quick stripes.

EASY DRESS-UP STENCILED TABLECLOTH
- **Purchase a stencil or make your own** by photocopying the design shown here. Resize to the scale you choose. If you choose to make your own stencil, tape the stencil plastic over the design and trace with a fine-tip permanent marking pen.
- **Cut out the design** with a crafts knife. Work on a self-healing mat, available at art supply or fabric stores.
- **Cut out paper watering cans** and pin to your tablecloth to help you place your stenciled motifs, if desired.
- **Practice stenciling** on a scrap of fabric first. Tape the stencil to the smooth, ironed scrap with stencil tape. (It's less tacky than regular tape.)
- **When you are pleased** with your scrap sample, proceed to stencil the tablecloth. Apply stencil paint with a stencil brush. Move firmly in a circular motion. Untape and carefully lift stencil in a quick motion.

DAISY STRAW HATS

SKILL LEVEL

Beginner

TIME

2 hours

SUPPLIES

- Plain, wide-brim straw hats
- Pencil
- Artist's paintbrush
- White and yellow acrylic paints
- Green sheer organza ribbon (at least 60 inches per hat)
- Hot-glue gun
- Glue sticks

DAISY TABLECLOTH OVERSKIRT

SKILL LEVEL

Beginner

TIME

3 hours

SUPPLIES

- Gauze fabric
- Fray-checking product
- Pencil
- Rubber foam
- Paper
- White and yellow fabric paint
- Two small paintbrushes

DAISY DAYS STRAW HATS

- **Hand-paint petals around brims of hats as shown.** If you are unsure of spacing, mark first with pencil so the petals are evenly spaced. Taper ends and paint white. Paint centers yellow. Cut ribbon in half and hot glue to hat for ties. Tie each hat with a generous bow around the back of the chair.
- **Secure tightly enough** so that the hat doesn't slip from the back of the chair.

DAISY DAYS TABLECLOTH OVERSKIRT

- **Cut a square of gauze** to comfortably fit your table. Unravel about ½ inch on each edge and run a line of fray-stopping product to prevent further unraveling. Carefully draw and cut out a 3-inch-diameter daisy from rubber foam.
- **Lay the fabric over paper.** Coat one side of the stamp with fabric paint. Carefully press the stamp down and lift up. Fill in with a small brush. Repeat for each flower. Space evenly over the table overskirt for a happily random, cheerful look.
- **Allow daisies to dry completely.** Paint the center of each daisy with yellow fabric paint. If you prefer, tamp yellow daisies and fill in with white centers. Or vary the sizes of the stamps with some larger, some smaller daisy motifs.

TIN CAN LUMINARIES

SKILL LEVEL

Beginner

TIME

2 hours

SUPPLIES

- 26-ounce cans
- Old-fashion beer can opener
- Work gloves
- Hammer
- Sharp nail
- Terra-cotta saucer
- Votive candles
- All-purpose glue (optional)

TIN CAN LUMINARIES

- **Remove labels, tops, and bottoms from 26-ounce cans.** Use an old-fashion beer can opener to make triangular holes around the perimeter of the top and bottom of each can. Wear work gloves; beware of sharp edges.
- **Using a hammer and a nail,** carefully punch additional holes in a pattern on the surface of each can. Aim for simple, stylized patterns. Work with a spare can or two for practice.
- **Place each can in a terra-cotta saucer** with a votive candle inside. For taller bases, glue a pair of saucers bottom to bottom. Vary the tall and short bases on your deck, patio, and tabletop for lively decorative interest.

BAMBOO TRELLIS AND VALANCE

SKILL LEVEL

Beginner

TIME

6 to 8 hours

TRELLIS SUPPLIES

- Bamboo
- Synthetic twine
- Scissors
- Handsaw
- Nails
- 1×2, length of wood to be determined
- Tape measure
- Pencil
- Masking tape

VALANCE SUPPLIES

- Bamboo
- Synthetic twine
- Scissors
- Tape measure
- Pencil
- Handsaw

BAMBOO TRELLIS AND VALANCE

■ **For the trellis, purchase bamboo** at specialty garden stores, some home centers, or online. The featured project uses 8-foot lengths of 2-inch-diameter bamboo and synthetic twine. Natural twine quickly deteriorates.

■ **Draw a diagram to scale to determine** the spacing and amount of needed bamboo. Nail a 1×2 board to the porch soffit to act as a brace to hold the top of the vertical bamboo in place. The bottom of the vertical bamboo rests on the ledge of the porch rail and is tied in placed with twine.

■ **Measure and mark** where horizontal pieces intersect with vertical pieces. Cut horizontal pieces to size, position, and tape in place. Lash the horizontals at each intersection with synthetic twine after removing the tape. This is a square lashing technique.

■ **The valance uses 1-inch-diameter bamboo,** tied together in 18-inch intervals. Cut bamboo to desired length. Lay the bamboo on a flat surface, alternating thicker and thinner ends. Lightly mark where bamboo will be tied and tie together using a series of knots. Hang the valance from large plant hooks.

SWINGING DAYBED

SKILL LEVEL

Advanced

TIME

2 to 3 days

SUPPLIES

- Twin-size mattress
- Tape measure
- Fabric for mattress cover
- Clear pine lumber
- Saw
- Wood glue
- Lag screws
- Drill and bits (including countersink bit)
- Wood plugs or wood filler
- Carpenter's square
- Miter box
- Finishing nails
- Sandpaper
- Stain or paint
- Eight eyebolts with nuts and washers
- Heavy-duty chain
- Hammer

SWINGING DAYBED

■ **Swing in style and comfort with this twin-size porch swing.** The featured project is a custom design crafted by Gerald and Patricia Little for Studio Remontant in Atlanta, GA, 404/874-2084. See below for a do-it-yourself project based on the Little's design.

■ **Purchase the mattress.** A standard twin mattress measures approximately 39 inches by 75 inches, but the size can vary slightly from one manufacturer to another. You may need to adjust the size of the swing to fit your mattress.

■ **Choose good-quality wood.** For ease of construction, stock wood sizes, such as 2×2, 2×4, and 2×6 are used. (Note that nominal wood sizes are bigger than the actual size of the wood. For example, a nominal 2×4 measures only 1½ x 3½ inches.) Select straight, warp-free pieces that are free of knots or other defects.

■ **Make sides first.** Begin by cutting four 2×4 legs, each 26 inches long. Cut four 2×6 apron pieces, each 31 inches long. (These are the horizontal boards—top and bottom—on the sides.) Attach two of the legs to two of the aprons using wood glue and lag screws. Pre-drill for the screws to prevent splitting the wood. Use carpenter's square to check all angles. Countersink the screw heads and plug. Note that the top apron is attached two inches down from the top of the legs and the lower apron two inches above the bottom of the legs. Make the second end to match the first. Allow glue to dry.

■ **Connect it all together.** Cut three 2×6 rails, each 75 inches long. With glue and lag screws,

attach one rail to the front of the two sides in line with the lower side aprons. Attach the two back rails to line up with the upper and lower aprons. Stagger the screw holes to miss the other lag screws. Check that everything is square and allow to dry.

■ **Cut 2×2 pickets to fit between the upper and lower aprons approximately 15 inches long.** Space the pickets evenly, using eight on each end and the remainder across the back. Install with glue and finishing nails. Countersink and fill all nail holes.

■ **Add supports for the seat.** Cut two 2×2 ledgers 75 inches long. Glue and nail these on the inside of the front and rear lower aprons, exactly ¾ inch from the top of the aprons. Cut six 1×6 slats 31 inches long and install on top of the ledgers.

■ **Sand the entire piece smooth.** Paint or stain the piece as desired. Light stains work best on pine. For an easy, no-drip job, use one of the new gel stains. Finish with two or three coats of clear polyurethane. For a painted finish, prime first, then apply two coats of exterior latex enamel.

■ **To hang the swing, install four eyebolts in the upper side aprons, a few inches in from the legs.** (Make sure the bolts miss the pickets.) Position the swing on the porch. Attach four more eyebolts to ceiling joists directly over swing eyebolts. If there are no joists correctly positioned, add 2×6 braces spanning existing joists and run eyebolts through the ceiling into braces. Never anchor directly to ceiling paneling or drywall. Make up four equal lengths of heavy chain to hold the swing about 3 inches off the floor.

CONSTRUCTION TIPS FOR SUCCESS

Adding a porch, deck, or terrace offers an economical way to increase your family's living space. Here are a few suggestions to guide you through the process.

■ **Consider the sun.** The way a porch or deck faces will determine whether it is an enjoyable place or a sunbaked wasteland. A porch on the south side of a house will provide shade during the hottest part of the day in summer. In winter, the lower sun can slide under the porch, making it a warm, inviting spot on a frosty day. A south-facing deck or terrace, however, will be hot in summer, unless you add an arbor or umbrella for shade. A deck or porch on the east side can be a delightful spot for morning coffee year-round, but it will be dark and cold on a winter's afternoon. A west-facing porch or deck can be hot in summer when the afternoon sun blasts in. A well-placed tree, screen, or roll-down blinds can be the cure. An outdoor space on the north side of your home will only get an hour or two of early morning and late afternoon sun in the summer. In winter, the house will block all direct sunlight.

■ **Catch a breeze.** For maximum effect, a porch or deck should be open on three sides to allow cross-ventilation. Add a ceiling fan to stir air on calm nights. If you plan on using in winter, add a hedge or outbuilding to screen winds.

■ **Size it up.** If you plan on using your porch, deck, or terrace for entertaining, size does matter. For sitting, a depth of 8 feet is the minimum. That allows enough room for a row of rockers and circulation space between the seating and the railing. If you will be using your deck or porch for casual dining or as a living area, allow at least 10 feet and preferably 12 feet of depth. Width is also important. One rule of thumb: a deck or porch should be at least as big as the room it opens off of. Sketch the furniture placement to scale on graph paper to make sure it will all fit.

■ **Keep to code.** For your safety, most local building codes place strict requirements on decks, porches, and balconies that are raised above ground level. Typically, any structure more than a certain height (usually 30 or 36 inches) above ground level must be fitted with a railing. The railing must be a minimum height (36 or 42 inches are typical requirements). Most codes also specify the spacing between the vertical balusters or pickets (a 4-inch minimum is common).

■ **Decking options.** Wood is by far the most popular choice for a raised deck or porch. Pressure-treated pine makes a long-lasting, economical surface; check to see if wood is kiln dried after treatment to minimize warping and twisting. Follow safety standards which include wearing long sleeves, nonabsorbent gloves, a dust mask, and safety goggles. Seal cut ends. More expensive options include cedar and redwood. Man-made substitutes include plastic lumber and composite wood decking, which is made from sawdust and recycled plastic. But color choices are limited. Synthetic decking lacks the warmth, variety, and splinters of real wood. Plastic lumber and composite decking are strictly for use as deck surfaces. Wood, preferably pressure-treated pine, should be used for the joists, beams, and posts that support the deck. Use concrete piers under the posts to eliminate potential rotting where a post enters the ground.

■ **Terrace or patio options.** For an on-grade terrace or patio, concrete, brick, and stone are the most popular. Concrete, usually the least expensive, can be stained, scored, or stamped to give a variety of looks. You can use brick for the entire surface or to edge concrete or gravel. A brick-on-sand patio makes an easy do-it-yourself project.

■ **Working with water.** For drainage, any exterior deck, patio, porch, or terrace needs to slope slightly. Usually a pitch of $\frac{1}{4}$ inch per foot will be enough to quickly carry off rainwater. Remember to slope a porch or deck away from the house; decking boards should run perpendicular to the house to direct water away from the foundation.

■ **Keep out the bugs.** Plastic insect screening is inexpensive and holds up well in almost any climate but can tear. For protection, add a second layer of screen below the rail. Or use a layer of wire mesh to reinforce the plastic screen. Protect screen doors as well. To prevent insect attacks from below, run screening over joists.

■ **Paint to last.** To increase the odds that your porch looks good for a long time, properly prepare and paint posts, railings, and other trim. All wood parts exposed to the weather should be back-primed before installation to minimize warping and rotting. Or use pressure-treated wood for trim. Wood that you plan to paint should be primed as soon as possible to improve adhesion. Waiting a few weeks can reduce the wood's ability to hold paint. Follow the primer with at least two coats of exterior paint. Don't cut corners; more expensive 100 percent acrylic latex paint will last longer and look better than cheaper alternatives.

CONTRIBUTORS/RESOURCES

**Pages 4-5, 28-37, 58-59, 61 (upper), 82, 83
(left), 93:** Katy Stoddard, regional contributor;
Emily Minton, photography
Pages 8-15: Elle Roper, photography

Pages 16-17: Lynn McBride, regional editor;
Gordon Beall, photography
Pages 18-23: Lynn McBride, regional editor;
Cheryl Dalton, photography
Pages 24-25: Tom Wilson, architect; Dianne
Carroll, regional editor; Jenifer Jordan, photography
Pages 26-27: Maureen O'Brien, design; Linda
Krinn, contributor; Ross Chapple, photography
**Pages 52-53, 56-57, 76-81, 83 (right), 92-93,
114-115:** Lynn Nesmith, regional contributor;
Emily Minton, photography
Page 54, 66, 68-69: Wade Scherrer, styling; Bill
Hopkins, photography
Page 67, 71, 150-151, 154, 156: Wade Scherrer,
styling; King Au, Studio Au
Page 83: Charlotte Comer, design; Mary Baskin,
regional editor; Jenifer Jordan, photography
Page 97: Charles Faudree, design; Nancy Ingram,
regional editor; Gordon Beall, photography
Pages 98-99: Gail Miller, design; Kristine Carber,
regional editor; Jamie Hadley, photography
Pages 102-103, 117: Ryan Gainey, design; Elle
Roper, regional contributor; Emily Minton
Pages 104-105: Susan Dowell, regional contrib-
utor; Gordon Beall, photography
Page 116 (left): Elaine Markoutsas, regional edi-
tor; James Yochum, photography
Pages 128-129, 132-133: Ginger Irby, design
and styling; Emily Minton, photography
Pages 135, 139 (left): Donna Talley Wendt,
regional contributor; Gordon Beall, photography
Page 136: Liberty & Sons, design; Mary Baskin,
regional editor; Jenifer Jordan, photography
Page 137: Elvin McDonald, design
Pages 142-145: Dianne Carroll, regional editor;
Jenifer Jordan, photography
Pages 146-149, 155, 158: Brian Carter, project
design and styling; Emily Minton, photography
Pages 152-153: Amy Queen, design; Joetta
Moulden, editor; Fran Brennan, photography
Page 157: Wade Scherrer, project design and
styling; Scott Little, photography

SPECIAL THANKS

Daryl and Robert Davis, Seaside, FL
Stacey Brady, Seaside, FL
Lynn Field Reddoch Interior Design, Seaside, FL
Lesa Rowe
Potager's, Santa Rose Beach, FL
L. Pizitz & Co. Home and Cottage Collection,
Seaside, FL
Ken and Maureen Luke
Cheryl Troxel and Ny Nunn

U.S. UNITS TO METRIC EQUIVALENTS

To Convert From	Multiply By	To Get
Inches	25.4	Millimeters (mm)
Inches	2.54	Centimeters (cm)
Feet	30.48	Centimeters (cm)
Feet	0.3048	Meters (m)

METRIC UNITS TO U.S. EQUIVALENTS

To Convert From	Multiply By	To Get
Millimeters	0.0394	Inches
Centimeters	0.3937	Inches
Centimeters	0.0328	Feet
Meters	3.2808	Feet